IMAGES
of America

REMEMBERING
EDGEWATER BEACH
HOTEL

OUTER DRIVE—15 MINUTES TO LOOP

OUTDOOR DANCE FLOOR
PRIVATE BATHING BEACH
SCREENED DINING PORCH

LAKE MICHIGAN

BERWYN
ENTRANCE
HOTEL'S 200
GAR

RE THAN A 1000 FEET BEACH PROMENADE

NORTH ESPLANADE

SHOPS

MAIN ENTRAN

9 HOLE
MASHIE
PUTTING
GOLF COURSE

CHILDREN'S
PLAYGROUND

SHOPS

SHERIDAN ROAD - U. S. ROUTE 41

TENNIS COURTS
ILLUMINATED FOR NIGHT PLAYING

HILDREN'S
AYGROUND

SKATING RINK
IN WINTER

GARDENS

EDGEWATER BEACH HOTEL ～ 5300 Block Sheridan Road ～ CHICAGO, ILLINOIS

Postcards like this were a great early marketing tool for the Edgewater Beach Hotel to get guests to make their friends back home envious and hopefully attract even more patrons. The back of this card reads: "World renowned for its superb location on Lake Michigan and the 5300 Block of Sheridan Road with more than a thousand feet of the finest beach and beach promenade, out-of-door dancing on a large marble floor. Every up to date convenience for summer or permanent guests. Gardens, children's playgrounds, tennis, and golf putting course. Its Marine dining room is unsurpassed." (Courtesy of the Edgewater Historical Society.)

ON THE COVER: Known as the Queen of the Lakefront, the Edgewater Beach Hotel was of of a kind. The cover image shows the second and larger tower of the complex as it appeared an iconic postcard image from the 1920s produced by the Grogan Photo Company of Dan Illinois. (Courtesy of the Edgewater Historical Society.)

IMAGES
of America

REMEMBERING EDGEWATER BEACH HOTEL

John Holden and Kathryn Gemperle

ARCADIA
PUBLISHING

Published by Arcadia Publishing
Charleston, South Carolina

Printed in the United States of America

Library of Congress Control Number: 2021937757

For all general information, please contact Arcadia Publishing:
Telephone 843-853-2070
Fax 843-853-0044
E-mail sales@arcadiapublishing.com
For customer service and orders:
Toll-Free 1-888-313-2665

Visit us on the Internet at www.arcadiapublishing.com

*To Benjamin Marshall, who envisioned what the Edgewater Beach
Hotel could be; to William E. Dewey, who made that vision a
reality; and to the men and women who worked at the hotel for
50 years and made it a truly special place for all who visited*

CONTENTS

ACKNOWLEDGMENTS

This book is an outgrowth of an exhibit that was mounted at the Edgewater Historical Society (EHS) museum and debuted in June 2016 on the 100th anniversary of the opening of the Edgewater Beach Hotel. It is being published in the 50th anniversary year of when the hotel's demolition was completed.

The EHS exhibit and this book were made possible by the society's extensive collection of photographs, postcards, brochures, menus, matchbooks, and other items the museum had gathered on Edgewater Beach.

Unless otherwise noted, all of the images in this book come from the society's collection, which has been carefully curated for years, especially by longtime EHS board member LeRoy Blommaert. The society's news articles on the hotel were also tremendous resources. Board member Marsha Holland, an indefatigable sleuth, played an outsized role in assisting in the research. Thanks also to all of the EHS board members, especially architect Thom Greene. Chuck Quint and Larry Rosen were indispensable thanks to their consistent technical support.

Writer Adam Langer's 1989 article for the Chicago Reader, "Edgewater Beach Memories," is the definitive oral history of those who stayed, played, and celebrated at the hotel, as well as those who worked there for many years. The article features a heartfelt and often hilarious series of recollections that are only briefly excerpted in this book. Thankfully, the original article can be read online in its entirety at www.edgewaterhistory.org.

Thanks also to John Cellini, a historian at the Edgewater Beach Apartments; Tony Dudek of Tribune Media; Peggy Glowacki at the University of Illinois at Chicago Library; and Alison Hinderliter of the Newberry Library. Many thanks to Tina and Elaine Travlos and Roberta Estes for sharing family photos. Thanks as well to Marlies Stanton, one of the hotel's few remaining living staff members, who shared memories and photographs, and to Kathy Cromwell Stanton and Dennis Stanton for facilitating contact with her. Special thanks to John Monahan and Greg Borzo.

Finally, a heartfelt thank you to Caroline Vickerson at Arcadia Publishing, who was always quick with answers to numerous questions and made this process a joy.

INTRODUCTION

Many of the things for which Chicago is most fondly remembered are those that the city only had for a relatively brief time.

The World's Columbian Exposition of 1893 put Chicago on the map of the world's great cities and spurred the City Beautiful movement during the gritty era of industrialization. The Century of Progress International Exposition of 1933 and 1934 was a bright moment during the Great Depression and also put a spotlight on Chicago's role in leading the world through the development of technology and science. Riverview, a honky-tonk amusement park, lasted for 63 years. It has been gone for over 50 years, yet its legend endures.

Then there was the Edgewater Beach Hotel, the nation's preeminent urban waterfront resort hotel. It stood for just over 50 years—from 1916 to 1967—despite its glory and remarkable role in so many chapters of Chicago and US history. During its heyday, it epitomized the luxury hotel with its painstaking attention to detail both in the beauty of its spaces and also an overall sense of festiveness. It truly was a grand hotel and held a unique place in the hearts of many Chicagoans and guests from all over the world.

The hotel was that rarest of birds, perhaps without equal anywhere in the world: a full-service beachfront resort hotel located in the heart of one of the world's great cities. To find its rivals in the mid-20th century, one would have had to travel outside the Midwest to Atlantic City, Palm Beach, or the islands of California. In its original incarnation, the Edgewater Beach Hotel had not only hundreds of well-appointed rooms (all with views of the city and/or lake), elegant lobbies and lounges, shops, restaurants, banquet rooms, and dance floors but also a golf course, tennis courts, strolling gardens, and—of course—an actual waterfront and beaches.

This was made possible thanks to the savvy acquisition of key lakefront property by two enterprising sons of Irish immigrant families who had the foresight to see that a swampy stretch of land could host more than the sand dunes that dominated the landscape.

The splendor of the hotel's design reflected the full flowering of the artistry of the architectural firm Marshall and Fox, which had already graced Chicago with the majestic Blackstone Hotel and would later be responsible for some of the city's other most luxurious and romantic locales, such as the Drake Hotel and the South Shore Country Club (now the South Shore Cultural Center). All of those creations, along with the Edgewater Beach Apartments, still exist and give visitors a sense of what it might have been like to walk the halls and grounds of the Edgewater Beach Hotel.

As Chicago's answer to Jay Gatsby, Benjamin Marshall was the firm's purveyor of not only beautiful architecture but also the glamorous lifestyle and joie de vivre of some of the exicting activities that took place in the hotel's hallowed spaces: big band orchestras, floor shows, and waterfront dancing under the moonlight. These were part and parcel of the countless millions of individual experiences that were enjoyed by visitors to the Edgewater Beach Hotel through weddings, honeymoons, reunions, proms, conventions, and other celebrations. Many of the world's most famous denizens stayed at the Edgewater Beach Hotel, including legends of sports, music, and movies. However, the hotel is perhaps most fondly remembered by the average people whose visits might have been some of the most elegant and luxurious moments of their strenuous lives. Many people still speak in almost reverent amazement about their parents celebrating weddings or honeymoons at the hotel.

The Edgewater Beach Hotel was also the backdrop for many amazing developments in American culture: it helped give rise to the Zenith Radio Company, some of the earliest radio broadcasts (including the launch of WGN Radio, the most powerful station in the Midwest), and two of the most influential radio broadcasters in the nation. It played a key role in spreading jazz and big band music. It was the site of one of the first luxury shopping arcades and the country's—perhaps the world's—first indoor parking garage. Talk about convenience! But it was its sheer elegance and outstanding service, orchestrated by longtime general manager William Dewey, that really made the hotel something special.

But as with Brigadoon, the glory of the Edgewater Beach Hotel was fleeting. Little remains beyond the fond memories of those who visited or worked there. We have attempted to gather some of those memories in this book to remind the world of the grandeur and excitement that were once available on the shore of Lake Michigan in the city of Chicago.

One

ORIGINS

During the early years of the 20th century, Edgewater, one of Chicago's newer and more prosperous communities, continued to build critical mass as an attractive and desirable place to live. Edgewater's founder and leading developer, John Lewis Cochran, acquired and subdivided much of the area for development. During the 1900s and 1910s, most of the area had been built out by a number of developers. Among these were John J. Corbett and John T. Connery, who had succeeded in buying most of the land along the shore of Lake Michigan between Berwyn and Bryn Mawr Avenues in the first decade of the century.

Various plans for the land were entertained, but the vision and clout to develop a world-class resort hotel did not come together until Corbett and Connery connected with the irrepressible Benjamin Marshall and his partner Charles Fox. In the first half of 1915, the Edgewater Beach Hotel Corporation was formed. The developers had a major incentive to get their new hotel constructed and open for business within a remarkably expedited timetable of just over a year. The hotel was booked with delegates for the 1916 Republican National Convention, which would be held in June.

From the beginning, the hotel enjoyed remarkable success. Its offerings included all the amenities of a first-class resort. In addition to the immensely popular swimming opportunities afforded by the lake, the resort also offered opportunities for golf, tennis, and strolling along the 1,000-foot-long Beach Walk. When the sun set and the action moved indoors, music, dancing, and fine dining were available in the Marine Dining Room, which would become the heart and soul of the complex.

The success of the initial 400-room hotel was so great that a few short years after it opened, the hotel's owners embarked upon an ambitious expansion. The over-the-moon plans of Marshall initially envisioned four additional Maltese cross–shaped structures north of the original hotel, culminating in a 2,000-room hotel at Bryn Mawr. This sprawling campus was also slated to include an enormous entertainment complex with spa facilities, a massive movie palace, and an enclosed jungle of 300 palm trees.

Ultimately, it was decided that the first expansion would be to the south of the original hotel building, where a 19-story, 600-room annex was constructed on the site of the original hotel's gardens.

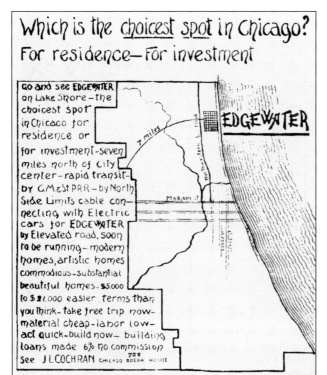

Which is the choicest spot in Chicago?
For residence—For investment

Go and see EDGEWATER on Lake Shore – the choicest spot in Chicago for residence or for investment—seven miles north of City center—rapid transit—by C.M.&St PRR—by North Side Limits cable connecting with Electric cars for EDGEWATER by Elevated road, soon to be running—modern homes, artistic homes commodious-substantial beautiful homes $5000 to $21,000 easier terms than you think—take free trip now—material cheap-labor low—act quick-build now—building loans made 6% no commission See J L COCHRAN CHICAGO OPERA HOUSE

EDGEWATER

The community of Edgewater was established by developer John Lewis Cochran in 1886 as an independent suburb before it was annexed by the City of Chicago in 1889. This map also serves as an advertisement for Cochran's suburb. Edgewater was an upscale community of single-family homes and residential apartments that attracted people from the city's burgeoning upper and middle classes, as well as numerous ambitious builders and talented architects.

While John Lewis Cochran purchased much of the land in Edgewater, he did not buy the lakeshore land where the hotel would be built, possibly because it was swampy and had no fixed eastern border in Lake Michigan. A road along the shore could not be paved because of the shifting landscape. Cochran drew rapid development to Edgewater by providing a link to direct rail service to downtown and widely advertising the convenience and desirability of his new suburb.

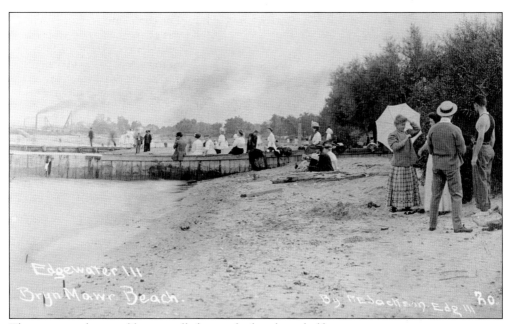

Edgewater Ill
Bryn Mawr Beach.   By P.E. Jackson. Edg Ill 20.

The property that would eventually house the hotel was half underwater when the property lines were drawn. The original shoreline of Edgewater was much like that of the rest of Chicago—sandy and swampy. The shaded area in the schematic at right shows where landfill was needed. Luxembourger farmers originally cultivated the surrounding area for raising vegetables. In 1908, local residents John Corbett and John Connery purchased land from Berwyn Avenue to just south of Bryn Mawr Avenue. In 1914, architect Benjamin Marshall purchased 300 feet of adjacent frontage. The combined properties of Corbett, Connery, and Marshall, which stretched to about 2,000 feet long and 300 feet across (at its widest point), cost roughly $750,000. Marshall then began planning with Corbett and Connery to build a unique urban resort hotel complex. Negotiations with the Lincoln Park Commission, which had control of Chicago's north lakefront, then began to resolve boundaries for the property in light of an irregular shoreline. Though their final agreement established an eastern property line in the submerged land, it did not give the developers riparian rights, the lack of which would cost the hotel its coveted waterfront location when Lake Shore Drive was later extended. In the above image, the smoke plumes in the background are from equipment landfilling for the hotel.

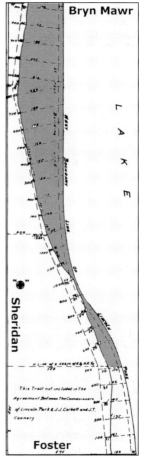

11

John J. Corbett,
The First President
Died June 27, 1919.

The Men Responsible for the Success of the Edgewater Beach Hotel.

John T. Connery,
Originally Treasurer
Now President

B. H. Marshall,
Vice President

Chas. E. Fox,
Secretary

W. M. Dewey,
Treasurer and
General Manager

Mr. Chas. E. Fox Died October 31, 1926 and Mr. Dewey is now Secretary-Treasurer and Managing Director, with George F. Getz and Milton J. Foreman as members of the Board of Directors.

The Edgewater Beach Hotel Company was formed on May 22, 1915, with four stockholders: John J. Corbett, president; John T. Connery, treasurer; Benjamin H. Marshall; and Charles E. Fox, secretary. Most fortunately for their venture, the group brought on Corbett's nephew, William Dewey, as general manager of the hotel. Corbett and Connery, both sons of Irish immigrants, joined forces in 1908 to purchase the future site of the Edgewater Beach Hotel. Corbett had plenty of experience as a builder. Connery was president of a coal company. As one of Chicago's most prolific architects and developers, Marshall played an outsized role in creating the Gilded Age environs of Chicago's monied classes. His work included the Blackstone and the Drake Hotel, the South Shore Country Club, and especially upscale lakefront apartment buildings. Marshall's work on the Blackstone convinced him that Chicago needed a hotel that could also offer all the amenities of a country club. Marshall was a high-caliber bon vivant. The Edgewater Beach Hotel was intended to be a principal site for the comings and goings of Chicago's high society. Architect Charles Fox, who did much of the actual design for Marshall's visions, was Marshall's partner for decades.

Though he was not initially an owner of the hotel, William E. Dewey, the nephew of John J. Corbett, had the most important role in making the Edgewater Beach Hotel the phenomenal success it would become. The hiring of Dewey might have been the most fortuitous example of nepotism in Chicago history, as his taste, attention to detail, general sense of showmanship, and skill at public relations all helped to build the hotel's impeccable reputation. Dewey is shown here just before his retirement with his four sons, all of whom served in the military in World War II.

This logo for the hotel emphasizes the Maltese cross form of the hotel and how it was surrounded by the lake and sailboats to the east and greenery to the north and south. It was used on all manner of accessories for the hotel, from china and ashtrays to matchbooks, maps, and stationery.

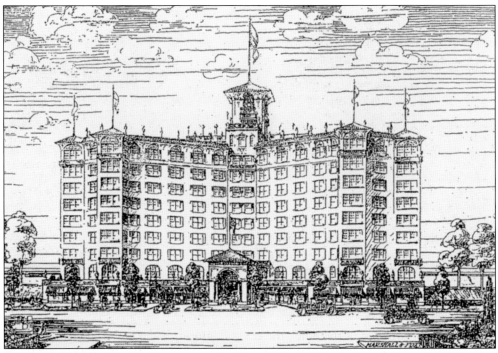

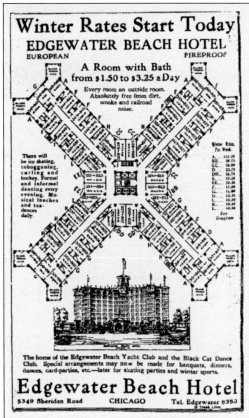

This 1915 rendering of the proposed new hotel emphasized its elegance and premier lakefront location. In October 1915, trust deeds were recorded totaling $728,500 for the financing of the hotel; the complex was later mortgaged for $3 million. It was promoted as "a sort of seaside annex to the Blackstone" hotel in downtown Chicago, and shuttle service between the two hotels was to be provided both by motorcoach and boat.

The floor plan of the Edgewater Beach Hotel was that of a Maltese cross (also known as a Greek cross), which has four arms of equal length. Each arm had an indentation at its end, creating two small nooks that added to corner floor space and views. Marshall and Fox would employ the same basic design motif for its future proposals at the site—those that were built and not built.

Prior to the construction of the hotel, the environs already had a posh pedigree. The land immediately south of the hotel land was home to the Saddle and Cycle Club, an exclusive riding club established in 1895. Though horseback riding no longer takes place there, the club has endured the area's dramatic changes and remains active and exclusive.

Work on the hotel by the Darling and Eitel construction company began in late spring 1915 and proceeded at a frenetic pace. The project took just about a year to complete. The total cost was about $3 million. On June 7, 1916, the Edgewater Beach Hotel welcomed its first guests—delegates to the Republican National Convention being held at the Chicago Coliseum. US Supreme Court justice Charles Evans Hughes was nominated to challenge incumbent president Woodrow Wilson. Though Hughes was narrowly defeated, the Edgewater Beach Hotel was successfully launched for its storied half-century run.

The often turbulent waters of Lake Michigan led to the constant shifting of the shoreline. Before anything could be built on the Edgewater Beach property, the developers had to create a fortified barrier on the eastern edge of their land.

Ransome Bantam Mixer laying sidewalk around Edgewater Beach Hotel, Chicago, Ill.
Albert Graff & Co., Contractors

Few images exist of the construction of the original Edgewater Beach Hotel tower. Here, cement crews are putting the finishing touches on the 1,000-foot-long Beach Walk, one of the hotel's most prominent features. This was the longest waterfront esplanade west of Atlantic City at the time and was a chief attraction for those looking to enjoy Chicago's lakefront breezes. This advertising image was produced by the Ransome Concrete Machinery Company to illustrate how its Bantam Mixer could handle even the biggest jobs.

The building of the hotel necessitated the construction of a massive seawall (shown on the left side of this image) to keep the waters at bay. Like almost all of Chicago's fabled 29-mile-long lakeshore, this section is completely man-made. Despite its name, the Edgewater Beach Hotel initially had no beach. The stepped concrete seawall, or revetment, provided the only access to the waters of Lake Michigan. Over the years, the natural water and sand flows of Lake Michigan created an ever-growing beach. The central background of the photograph shows a short pier and diving platforms, which provided for additional water sports fun.

The stair-stepped revetment held the waters of Lake Michigan at bay. It also provided bathers with easier access to the lake. Piers along the revetment gave boaters easy access to the hotel property.

Partly in response to the growing prevalence of communicable diseases, including the Spanish flu, the early years of the 20th century brought on a boom in healthy outdoor activities in the United States, especially swimming. Until public beaches became more popular in later years, swimming was largely considered an activity of the wealthy at places such as the Edgewater Beach Hotel.

Strict decency codes were mandatory for all public bathing facilities at the time, including for patrons of the Edgewater Beach Hotel. Use of the waterfront at the hotel property was exclusively for hotel guests, a fact that prompted an ultimately futile legal challenge by neighbors west of the hotel property who did not want to lose their lake access.

This image of bathers at the hotel from the early 1920s shows a small sliver of beach forming along the revetment. The natural flows of the lake's water and sands—as well as the addition of new fill to the south and fluctuating lake levels—would eventually create an even more substantial beach alongside the hotel that would reach its peak in the late 1940s.

This view overlooking the original hotel building reveals its Maltese cross design. The hotel had 400 guest rooms, several dining rooms, and numerous lounges. To the north of the hotel, trees were planted along the lakeshore seawall. Just to the west was a nine-hole "putting green" golf course. Farther north, a wide walkway led to tennis courts. Beyond the tennis courts were homes built before plans were developed for the hotel; these homes were demolished in the 1920s to make way for the expanded Edgewater Beach complex.

The South Lawn as it appeared at the opening of the Edgewater Beach Hotel in June 1916 featured a walking path, gardens, trees, gazebos, and seating for visitors. It also featured a children's playground, which was later moved to the north side of the hotel. Lovely as it was, the entire South Lawn lasted less than a decade before it gave way to the construction of the hotel annex.

The porte cochere, or portico, provided protection from the elements for guests arriving at the hotel. Facing directly onto Sheridan Road, this grand entryway set the stage for the elegance that would be found throughout the rest of the hotel. It became one of the most famous features of the hotel and even found its way into national advertising campaigns for automobiles.

SCENE ON SHERIDAN RD.
AT EDGEWATER BEACH HOTEL, CHICAGO.   2936 ⓢ

The Edgewater Beach Hotel was located on the 5300 block of North Sheridan Road. Sheridan remains one of the most prestigious streets in Chicago and runs well north of the city limits to the Wisconsin border and beyond. Chicago's North Shore suburbs are home to the fanciest homes and estates. The street also features a number of other prestigious institutions, including Loyola University, Northwestern University, and the Bahá'í House of Worship.

This view of the hotel looking north on Sheridan Road was the perhaps most iconic image of the hotel and was the most popular subject for postcards in its early years.

Patrons of the Marine Dining Room would descend a grand staircase to make a grand entrance into what was the grandest space of the hotel. The elaborate entrance also provided opportunities for diners to see who was coming and going at one of Chicago's best places to see and be seen.

The centerpiece of the hotel was the Marine Cafe, later known as the Marine Room or Marine Dining Room, a gazebo-like structure located between the two eastern wings of the hotel. It had a 1,750-square-foot main floor for dining and dancing and tiered wings for additional dining areas overlooking the main floor. French doors opened onto the lakeside terrace. The Marine Room also had a retractable ceiling. Over the years, the room became a legendary Chicago locale and hosted many of the hotel's most memorable gatherings. It went through numerous changes over the years.

One of the most significant early events at the hotel was the November 1919 wedding of John Connery's daughter, which was held in the Marine Dining Room. Following the death of John Corbett that year, Connery took over as president of the hotel and retained that position until he died in 1937. The reception was huge, and everybody who knew the family was invited to an elaborate and elegant meal with music provided by an orchestra. The hotel served as the site for a countless number of Chicago's most elegant weddings over the decades.

Off the main lobby was a guest lounge that offers a glimpse of the atmosphere of the hotel when it first opened. Its elegant simplicity would be eclipsed by the palatial lounge areas created in the hotel's expansion.

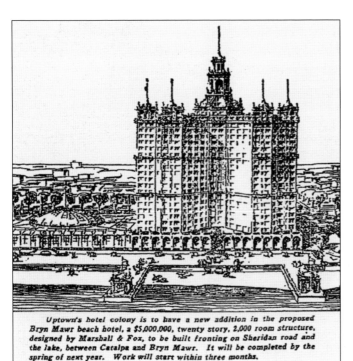

Uptown's hotel colony is to have a new addition in the proposed Bryn Mawr beach hotel, a $5,000,000, twenty story, 2,000 room structure, designed by Marshall & Fox, to be built fronting on Sheridan road and the lake, between Catalpa and Bryn Mawr. It will be completed by the spring of next year. Work will start within three months.

Not long after the hotel opened, its success drove Benjamin Marshall to dream even bigger dreams for the site. In 1920, he unveiled plans to create what would have been the largest resort complex in the world by building a series of four additional Maltese cross–shaped structures, culminating in a massive 2,000-room hotel at the southeast corner of Sheridan Road and Bryn Mawr Avenue. The other facilities were to include a men-only apartment hotel and entertainment venues, including an enormous new movie palace, as well as an enclosed garden that was supposed to house 300 palm trees.

Benjamin Marshall sold off many of his other holdings, including Gold Coast luxury apartment buildings, to fund his ambitious plan for the massive complex. When that plan faltered for lack of sufficient funding, in 1923, he instead proposed an addition to his existing hotel that grew into a 600-room, 19-story space that opened the following year.

The groundbreaking for the annex was held in March 1923. Land that was infilled just a decade earlier for the hotel campus was now being excavated to make way for the much larger addition that would complete the Edgewater Beach Hotel complex. The water in the excavation hole reflects the high water table at the site. A pile driver is installing wood pilings to support the new tower's foundation and the structure connecting it to the original building.

The Edgewater Beach complex was built by the construction firm of Darling and Eitel, which also built the nearby Riviera Theater and the Broadway Armory buildings, among other major structures in the community.

The hotel expansion's massive concrete foundation had to accommodate not only the new tower but also the underground parking garage, which provided the base for a structure linking the two towers. Like the first building, the annex was steel-framed. Its exterior walls were made of two layers of hollow-core clay blocks. These were overlaid with an exterior layer of brick. Finally, a layer of sand-colored parging was applied. The floors were formed with poured-in-place concrete with steel reinforcing bars. The same construction methods were used on the Edgewater Beach Apartments, which were built four years later in 1927.

Steel-frame construction, pioneered in Chicago near the end of the 19th century, allowed for unprecedented speed in erecting large buildings. Setbacks on the hotel's 10th and 18th floors gave the annex its distinctive "wedding cake" profile. When it was originally proposed, the annex was to have been seven stories shorter. The central tower was heightened for added capacity, which was prompted by booming business. Like the original building, the annex was crowned with matching cupolas and pyramidal roofs, visually tying the complex into an integrated whole.

By any measure, the Edgewater Beach annex was built at a breakneck pace in just under a year. Elevent months after its groundbreaking, the annex opened for business in February 1924. The new tower's 600 rooms brought the Edgewater Beach Hotel's total capacity to 1,000 rooms, making it the largest hotel in Chicago—for a short time. The exterior of the entire complex was a sandy beige hue, which Benjamin Marshall intended to complement Lake Michigan's spectacular sunrises and the adjacent sands.

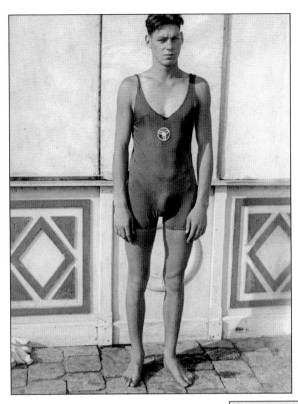

Among the earliest celebrity happenings at the hotel was a September 1922 competition in which 19-year-old swimming star Johnny Weissmuller tied the world record for the 50-yard race despite the rough waters of Lake Michigan. Weissmuller later achieved worldwide fame for winning five gold medals at the 1924 and 1928 Olympics. He became even more famous in the 1930s when he took on the role of Tarzan in a dozen films. The hotel also hosted a number of important tennis matches, bringing a number of stars of that sport to the hotel.

By the mid-1920s, the Edgewater Beach Hotel had developed a reputation as one of Chicago's most elegant and exciting entertainment destinations. A diving platform the hotel erected on the waterfront became its focal point for "fun in the sun." For the next 40 years, the hotel was the base of many of Chicago's most cherished memories.

Two

A Hotel Like No Other

The entrance to the hotel was through a stately portico that faced onto Sheridan Road. Inside, visitors were greeted by an elegant foyer with a winding staircase festooned with fresh-cut flowers. At the top of the stairs was the main lobby of the hotel. Straight across the lobby from the entrance was the Marine Dining Room, which faced directly onto the lake.

On the right side of the lobby was the hallway connecting the two main buildings. Far from an ordinary hallway, this 177-foot-long connecting corridor—which Benjamin Marshall christened the Passaggio—was a grand space unto itself and featured handsome hand-painted wooden beamed ceilings. Halfway down, the Passaggio was flanked by two grand spaces: the East Lounge and the West Lounge. Each boasted cathedral ceilings, ample windows to allow in natural light, and elegant seating areas where guests could socialize. The ground floors of the annex tower also contained a wide variety of banquet rooms and gathering spaces like the massive Grand Ballroom, which could accommodate a dinner for 1,000 attendees, and intimate rooms for smaller gatherings of families and friends.

The Passaggio and the lounges sat atop a 200-space parking garage, which was perhaps the first of its kind in the nation. This feature was a key attraction for appealing to an increasingly car-dependent society and those wishing to directly enter the complex in inclement weather.

Fronting the Passaggio structure at street level was an arcade of shops that could be accessed from inside the hotel as well as from the street. These elegant boutiques provided an offering of all the items and services that any vacationer might need without ever having to leave the hotel.

But the hotel's ultimate glamour was to be found on its outdoor band shell and marble dance floor—the only one of its kind. Dancing under the stars was truly the main attraction at the Edgewater Beach Hotel, even if the season for such activity only lasted for a few months each year.

One of the most famous features of the Edgewater Beach Hotel was the portico, which faced Sheridan Road. It served as the public face of the hotel and the gateway to the glorious interior. It was an extraordinarily busy location throughout the hotel's history, with private cars, limousines, and shuttle buses continuously coming and going.

Inside the main entrance of the hotel was a lovely foyer bracketed by two winding staircases that led guests to the main reception area of the hotel. Between the staircases was the entrance to two of the hotel's most popular venues, the Black Cat Room and the Yacht Club, both fashionable with younger clientele.

This was one of the most popular postcards of Edgewater Beach, highlighting the importance of floral displays around the hotel. Placing the main reception area at the top of a staircase leading from street level was a design Benjamin Marshall also used at the Blackstone and, later, the Drake Hotel—both in Chicago.

The lobby sat at the center of the hotel's Maltese cross floor plan, making it the focal point of the main floor and providing access to wings of the hotel. From this central vantage point, one could look down each of the four wings of the hotel. The lobby manager controlled a small empire of 20 to 30 employees, including bellhops and elevator operators, who offered guests tips about upcoming activities at the hotel.

Luxuriously appointed elevators were staffed by operators around the clock. The hotel also had a busy newsstand selling Chicago's multiple morning and afternoon newspapers and other essentials.

An enormous bank of private pay-phone booths was located off the main lobby, providing guests the convenience of being able to make private telephone calls. Note the wooden doors and alcove-type space away from the noise of the main lobby. The phones were available to hotel and restaurant guests.

EDGEWATER BEACH YACHT CLUB
EDGEWATER BEACH HOTEL
5300 BLOCK – SHERIDAN ROAD
CHICAGO, ILLINOIS.

The Yacht Club was the most iconic tavern in the hotel complex and endured through myriad changes at the hotel. George Stanton, a chief executive steward at the hotel, offered this description: "The nautically themed venue was accessed by coming down a gangplank. Its porthole-shaped windows looked out directly at Lake Michigan. It even had canvass walls which would undulate under the influence of simulated winds. It was made up to look like the inside of a ship. You'd walk in . . . and when you hit a certain spot, it blew a whistle like a yacht. It was so unique."

Black Cat Room- Main Building
Available for Conventions, Dinners
Luncheons, etc.
Edgewater Beach Hotel, Chicago.

This 1930s photograph shows the entrance to the Black Cat Room, a dining and dancing space located on the hotel's ground floor. Originally called the Black Cat Dance Club, it was a sibling to the picturesque Yacht Club. The first social event held at the hotel was a DePaul University senior class prom held in the Black Cat Room. Many college and high school social events were held there, and it was the hotel's liveliest entertainment venue in the 1920s and 1930s. It was especially popular with students from Northwestern University, which was located six miles north on Sheridan Road in alcohol-free Evanston.

Passaggio·Edgewater Beach Hotel
Chicago, Ill.

Providing access between the two towers of the complex required a long connecting corridor roughly 180 feet long. But in Benjamin Marshall's deft hands, simply walking between the two buildings became an event in itself via the beautifully detailed and furnished Passaggio. Halfway down its length, the Passaggio was flanked by two cavernous lounges.

FIREPLACE, EDGEWATER BEACH HOTEL, 5300 BLOCK SHERIDAN ROAD, CHICAGO. 104406

The West and East Lounges, which straddled the Passaggio, were intended to be gathering places for hotel guests. These elegant lounges were decorated in the Spanish Baroque style. The wood-beamed ceilings were covered in decorative painted scrollwork. A large arched window flanked by decorative columns accentuated the far end of the room. The windows at the lower level and the clerestory windows just below the roofline provided an abundance of natural light. These spaces were often used for weddings, receptions, and, later, conventions and trade show activities.

This four-sided fireplace rose to a full two stories and was the visual centerpiece of the two-story West Lounge. It was also the focal point of numerous social gatherings and the iconic subject of many photographs and postcards. It signaled that while the hotel was grand, it also had a certain coziness.

Fireplace - West Lounge
Edgewater Beach Hotel
Chicago, Ill.

East Lounge
Beach Hotel

The Edgewater Beach Hotel was an enormously popular subject for postcards, perhaps because Chicago was the leading center for postcard production in the first half of the 20th century. The high-arched ceiling provided a dramatic visual element that connected the two lounges.

Henry Weiner
Studio
Imported Hangings
Tapestries
Petit Point Bags, etc. etc.

Edgewater
Beach
Drug Store

E. Rohde's
Beauty Shop
and corps of
expert operators

Nonette
Hat Shop
Miss Nonie Ervin,
Mgr.

Susy Collin Miller
Shop
Gowns, Wraps, etc.

Edgewater
Beach
Gift
Shop

Edna Wheaton
Shop
Children's
Apparel
and
Accessories

Edgewater Beach Needlecraft Shop
Mrs. Marie Riske, Prop.

Marti

Do Your Christmas Shopping in the Edgewater Beach Hotel Shops—Park your Car in Our

EDGEWATER BEACH
HOTEL DELIVERY

Purchases made in our shops
will be delivered to your door.

The flower shop offered a wide selection of arrangements and included delivery to facilitate floral room service. The shop, originally on the same level as the lobby, was one of the most popular at the hotel. When color printing became widely available, color postcards from the flower shop became popular images. This is the delivery truck for the floral shop, which not only served hotel guests but also the surrounding community.

Edgewater
Beach Hotel
Flower Shop

Edgewater Beach
Studio
Studio and "At Home"
Portraiture
Leon Glass-Proprietor

The Boudoir Shop
Lingerie, Negligees
Accessories
Marian Capen-
Myrtle Hutchinson

~ Mens' Wear

d avoid crowds and delays.

This 1920s montage from the hotel's in-house magazine, *Ripples* (which was printed at the hotel), shows the wide array of shops, services, and other amenities available for hotel guests and the general public. Besides dispensing prescriptions, the drugstore had a luncheonette and a postal station. The shopping arcade between the two buildings allowed for stores that could be accessed from an inside arcade and from the street. This was among the earliest indoor shopping arcades in the nation and presaged the shopping and strip malls that would later dominate the retail industry in the United States.

This shop was owned and operated by Edgewater resident Emil Rohde. It provided for every beauty need, including manicurists and hairdressers. Rohde also invented Drene, the world's first synthetic shampoo that added a luster and shine to hair. In the 1930s, he sold Drene to Proctor & Gamble, which then rolled it out to consumers across the nation. Rohde was also known for consulting on the care of hair. He operated the salon until the early 1940s, when he sold it to an operator from Oak Park, Illinois. (Courtesy of Duke University.)

In Chicago

at Rohde's
in the Edgewater Beach Hotel

In Chicago, as in Paris, New York or London, you will find this complexion beautifying treatment in the smartest beauty shops.

An Edgewater Beach wedding and reception was the dream of many, and the photographer's studio on site was available to memorialize such events. The unidentified handsome couple in this undated wedding portrait, likely from the 1920s, was photographed in the studio.

Weddings were not the only occasions memorialized at the hotel's photography studio; family portraits were also popular. The family pictured here is unidentified but clearly decked out in their Sunday best for their visit to the hotel. Although their dour looks may suggest a less-than-happy time, subjects of group photographs in this era avoided smiling so as not to ruin images that required long exposure times.

As the Marine Dining Room grew in popularity, its decor was enhanced with decorative murals and the addition of a small jungle of potted ferns. The improvements gave the room an exotic flair and reflected the meticulous attention to detail of the hotel manager, William Dewey, who was known for his lavish decorations to fit various seasonal themes or for the floor shows in the Marine Dining Room.

Holidays were an especially festive time at the hotel, as illustrated by the Christmas decorations and canopy of lights in the center of the Marine Dining Room. The holiday festivities culminated with a huge New Year's Eve party that, over the years, became the place in Chicago for the smart set to welcome the new year. Each party featured an elegant dinner, a floor show, and music and dancing until the wee hours. A special keepsake menu was printed along with the program for the dance numbers.

Weddings were big business at the Edgewater Beach Hotel. This design for a wedding features an elaborate aisle and a raised platform for the altar. Half columns and ropes define the aisle. This arrangement is in one of the grand lounges. The reception would have been held in another room in the hotel. The Crystal Ballroom, located on the main floor of the hotel's annex, was the largest single space in the hotel and could accommodate 1,500 people.

Marketing materials for the hotel provided scores of photographs to give prospective patrons a sense of how elegant their events could be. This wedding design features a unique diorama with dolls (in the center of the photograph, above the candles) standing in for the bridal party. Also visible are the monogrammed Edgewater Beach Hotel china, silver service, and glassware. The tables, covered in floor-length cloths, are set up for a buffet-style dinner.

The kitchen's pastry department was second to none. This marketing photograph shows one of the many master pastry chefs standing by one of his lavish creations, which looks too beautiful to slice.

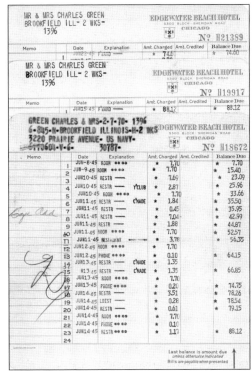

Bills for service were compiled on receipt cards. This was the bill for a two-week honeymoon at the Edgewater Beach Hotel in June 1945. The total charges for all services, including the room, restaurant meals, room service, telephone calls, and laundry, came to $190, which would be about $2,850 in 2021 dollars. This patron was a member of the US Navy at the time and reportedly got a nice discount as a result.

There were many choices available for banquet meals and events such as weddings, birthday and anniversary parties, bar mitzvahs, and corporate events. The kitchen featured a team of working chefs and menu planners who could meet any and every need. The hotel was especially known for its salads and pastries and even published its own book of salad recipes.

The hotel had a number of smaller rooms that could host a variety of functions, such as a family-style dinner or special group luncheon. Notices in newspaper society pages suggest that the hotel did a booming business hosting bridge clubs, ladies' groups, and other social events in these rooms. The hotel so adroitly took on the functions of a country club that it doomed the business of the community's actual country club, which was located two blocks away.

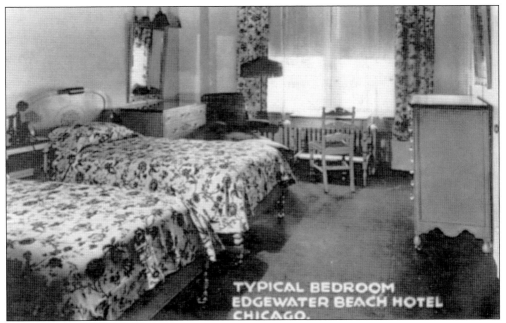

This image shows a typical room at the Edgewater Beach Hotel. The rooms were arranged to maximize the views of the lake as well as downtown Chicago and the complex's gardens, golf course, and other amenities.

In addition to the lounges on the main level, each floor of the hotel featured lounge areas for guests in the corner niches of the eastern wings. These provided lovely lakeshore views and breezes and allowed people to socialize with other guests without ever leaving their floor.

The hotel was planned with many dining rooms and several bars and restaurants. The Colonnade Room was for more casual dinners and lunches. Before Prohibition, it served cocktails with top-shelf liquor. It had a separate menu that was more budget-friendly than the hotel's other options but, nevertheless, had linen tablecloths. Its trade drew heavily on locals. The room was bright and airy and looked out on the waterfront.

To shuttle patrons to the downtown area, the hotel had its own fleet of motor coaches. Limousine service was available to a variety of Loop destinations, especially Marshall Field's Department Store. Fine vehicles from luxury automakers such as Mercedes-Benz were utilized. Guests could access the service under the portico at the main entrance.

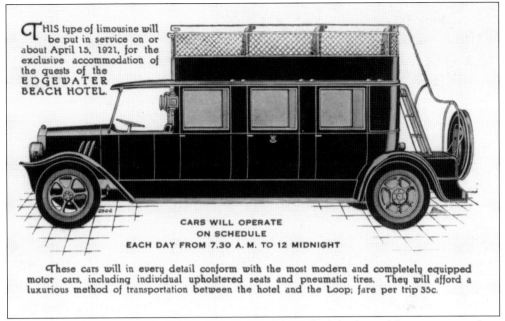

THIS type of limousine will be put in service on or about April 15, 1921, for the exclusive accommodation of the guests of the EDGEWATER BEACH HOTEL.

CARS WILL OPERATE
ON SCHEDULE
EACH DAY FROM 7.30 A. M. TO 12 MIDNIGHT

These cars will in every detail conform with the most modern and completely equipped motor cars, including individual upholstered seats and pneumatic tires. They will afford a luxurious method of transportation between the hotel and the Loop; fare per trip 35c.

Limousine service from the hotel was frequent, as this schedule shows. The service ran from 9:30 in the morning until midnight, meaning hotel guests could be shuttled to morning business meetings or back home after a night out on the town.

The Chicago Motor Coach company was the principal public bus transit service on Chicago's north lakefront starting in the 1910s and through the 1940s, when it was absorbed into today's Chicago Transit Authority. The Edgewater Beach Hotel was one of the most popular stops on its route.

One of the most innovative features of the addition to the hotel was the 200-space parking garage under the complex, which was promoted as of the first of its kind not only in Chicago but in the world. Management touted the complex as "the motorists' Mecca." Ironically, the onslaught of car culture in post–World War II America was a major contributing factor in the hotel's demise. The gasoline pumps at left highlight how fill-up service was also available at the hotel—a perk that would not be allowed under modern building codes. The importance of on-site parking at the hotel was driven in part by Chicago's ban on street parking. Previously, vehicles of guests had to be parked in private garages and lots throughout the nearby area. Ironically, the City of Chicago dropped its prohibition on street parking in 1924, the same year the Edgewater Beach Hotel garage opened. The entrance to the garage is at far right in the below image.

EDGEWATER BEACH HOTEL
5300 Block—Sheridan Road (U. S. Route 41), Chicago
Showing Location of 200-Car Garage

The availability of the parking garage and its fees were a prominent feature of advertising for the hotel for years after the annex opened—evidence of the growing primacy of the automobile in leisure travel. The garage also provided a key staging area for the Chicago Auto Show, which was held at the hotel for a number of years in the postwar era. Decades later, the Edgewater Beach Hotel was eventually surrounded by budget motels that had convenient parking as their stock in trade.

The hotel offered commuters and thrill-seekers the chance "for the most wonderful ride you'll ever have" along Chicago's fabled lakefront in the hotel's "hydro-aeroplane." The cost for this novel thrill in the early days of aviation was $10 for a single passenger ($131 in 2021 dollars). Decades later, the hotel offered guests helicopter service to O'Hare International Airport via a landing pad on the hotel's roof.

As part of Benjamin Marshall's vision for tying the Edgewater Beach Hotel to the clientele of the Blackstone and other downtown points, commercial boat service was established to whisk guests along the lakefront in as little as 15 minutes without the risks of traffic congestion. This service was also a selling point for the Edgewater Beach Apartments, which are shown here with the docks that facilitated this service.

This popular early photograph of the entire Edgewater Beach Hotel complex shortly after completion shows its various amenities, including its golf course and tennis courts. The one element it does not show is an actual beach, which did not exist when the hotel first opened. Over the next several decades, natural forces would create acres of beach in front of the hotel.

Three

THE PEOPLE WHO ENJOYED THE HOTEL AND THOSE WHO MADE IT RUN

The Edgewater Beach Hotel was the place to see and be seen. Not only did it attract vacationers from around the world, it was also the site for a wide variety of gatherings among the socialite set that ranged from weddings to bridge clubs. The hotel hosted many card clubs. For a lot of people, the hotel was a de facto country club—so much so that the nearby Edgewater Country Club was driven out of business by the competition.

Over the years, the hotel hosted thousands of events that ranged from weddings, proms, and corporate and professional dinners to truly unique gatherings such as circus performances and spectacular floor shows.

The hotel also became well-known as a place to see the famous. Regular denizens of the hotel included numerous bandleaders who played its stages, many of whom were then becoming household names through the miracle of radio. Given the hotel's relative proximity to Wrigley Field, home of the Chicago Cubs, it also became one of the most frequent places for visiting teams to stay. Casey Stengel and Yogi Berra tied one on until the wee hours at the Edgewater Beach Hotel. Politicians and performers of the stage, radio, and screen were frequent guests. Singer Bing Crosby was a semiregular, and his movie sidekick Bob Hope also stayed at the hotel.

The operations of the hotel were powered by a small army of employees that exceeded 1,000 at its peak, including reception clerks, bellboys, housekeepers, groundskeepers, waitstaff, bartenders, chefs, cooks, and concierges. The employees were diverse and included Black people and Japanese Americans, whose employment at the hotel offered them a ticket out of the internment camps.

Overseeing this vast operation was an improbable impresario of hospitality, William Dewey. His vision for a truly elegant and special place was the guiding light for the hotel for over three decades and cemented the reputation of the Edgewater Beach Hotel as a must-visit place. Though Dewey acquired his position at the hotel through a family connection and had no background in hospitality, he epitomized attention to detail. He was to hospitality what Marshall Field was to retail.

Every week saw scores of social gatherings and banquets taking place at the hotel. This 1932 event was a banquet for an amateur bowling league sponsored by the trade association of furriers. Many companies and trade associations sponsored bowling teams in the 1920s and 1930s.

This picture features one of many fashion shows held at the hotel by various groups as fundraising events. The North End Women's Club held several fashion shows to raise money to purchase a home north of the hotel on Sheridan Road as their center of operations. The group, which was founded in Edgewater, became part of the suffragist movement and later took on charitable work for the international anti-hunger group CARE.

As part of his efforts to make the hotel a family-friendly destination, general manager William Dewey planned three children's events each summer on the dance platform of the Beach Walk. Shows included circus performers, including acrobatic acts and live animals. This circus show took place in the Marine Dining Room in 1920.

Some of these Victor Adding Machine Company executives gathered in the hotel's Crystal Ballroom may look somber, as this photograph was taken on December 8, 1941, the day the United States entered World War II after the bombing of Pearl Harbor. Note that even business functions at the Edgewater Beach Hotel required formal wear. (Courtesy of Andrew Clayman.)

Even though the Edgewater Beach Hotel was far north of the 1933 Century of Progress World's Fair on Northerly Island, it still benefited handsomely from the boom in tourism. In order to help battle the impact of the Great Depression, Pres. Franklin Roosevelt ordered the World's Fair to remain open for a second year, providing a much-needed boost in business to all of Chicago's hotels.

The hotel also hosted the National Governors Association, which brought the governors of all 48 states to the hotel. William Dewey (right) is pictured here with Dwight Green, who served as governor of Illinois from 1941 to 1949. According to chief executive steward George Stanton, "The governors were a happy-go-lucky bunch. They wanted an American menu. Steak one night. Prime rib the next. We had to make a thousand steaks or a thousand prime ribs." This undated photograph is likely from the late 1940s.

The Edgewater Beach Hotel was the site of many patriotic activities during World War II. Women's groups would meet at the hotel weekly to sew for the armed services. Manager William Dewey made certain that sailors from the Great Lakes Naval Training Center in North Chicago were cared for. This group of sailors was enjoying Thanksgiving celebrations in the Yacht Club. (Courtesy of *Chicago Tribune* Archive/TCA.)

High school proms were another staple activity at the hotel. Shown here in the late 1950s are students from nearby St. Gregory's Catholic High School enjoying their big night out in the Polynesian Village. Future First Lady, US senator, and Secretary of State Hillary Rodham Clinton was among the high school students who attended proms at the hotel.

Much of the Edgewater Beach Hotel's fame came about due to its rich and famous guests, including the leading athletes, movie stars, and politicians of the day. Among the guests frequently cited are Franklin Delano Roosevelt, Dwight Eisenhower, Cary Grant, Charlie Chaplin, Frank Sinatra, Bette Davis, Marilyn Monroe, Jack Dempsey, the King of Saudi Arabia, and Mahatma Gandhi. Some of these reports are likely apocryphal; for instance, Gandhi never even visited the United States. One guest of the 1940s was musical comedy star Carmen Miranda, "the lady in the tutti frutti hat."

Shirley Temple was the child star who saved the 20th Century Fox film studio from bankruptcy and was the No. 1 box office draw in 1937 and 1938. In June 1938, Temple and her entourage stayed at the Edgewater Beach Hotel. She traveled the country that year promoting two of her biggest hits, *Rebecca of Sunnybrook Farm* and *Little Miss Broadway*.

Barbara Stanwyck and Robert Taylor were Hollywood's most glamorous couple in the 1940s. Though Taylor was a major star, he gave up his film career to join the war effort and served as a flight instructor for the US Naval Air Forces, which often brought him to the Great Lakes Naval Training Center and the Edgewater Beach Hotel. Stanwyck would visit him there during breaks in her busy film career.

Although they never stayed at the hotel at the same time, big-screen comedy partners Bing Crosby and Bob Hope both stayed at the hotel. Crosby stayed at the hotel on multiple occasions, including in April 1947. Crosby reportedly often attended Mass at nearby St. Ita's Catholic Church and made a substantial contribution for its new organ. Hope stayed at the hotel when he came to town to provide color commentary for the goings-on at the 1952 Republican National Convention.

Given its proximity to Wrigley Field, home of the Chicago Cubs, the Edgewater Beach Hotel frequently provided accommodations for visiting teams. Most memorably, Babe Ruth, the Bronx Bomber, stayed there on September 30, 1932, the night before hitting his infamous "called shot" homer at Wrigley during the World Series. Cubs fans do not need to be reminded which team went on to win the series that year. Ruth (right) is shown here with teammate Lou Gehrig.

Girl Fan Wounds Philly Ball Player Seriously

'Thrill Of Killing' Is Reason Given By Typist For Action

CHICAGO, June 15 (UP)—First Baseman Eddie Waitkus of the Philadelphia Phillies fought for life today after being shot by an apparently demented girl fan who said she planned for two years to kill him because "I was infatuated with him and wanted the thrill of murdering him."

Ruth Steinhagen, 19, typist for a Chicago insurance firm, admitted shooting the veteran National League star with a .22 caliber rifle in a room at the exclusive Edgewater Beach Hotel on the Chicago north shore.

Dreamed Of Killing

The girl, who is 5 feet, 10 inches tall, said she had been under treatment by two psychiatrists recently.

Sgt. Nick Reidy of the homicide detail said that the 29-year-old Waitkus "never knew that for the last two years he has lived with the threat of death constantly hanging over him."

"The girl said she sat in the stands off first base every Saturday and Sunday, while Mr Waitkus was with the Cubs in 1947 and 1948, dreaming of how she would kill him," Mr. Reidy said.

The girl admitted that she never had spoken to Mr. Waitkus up until the time last night when she sent a note luring him into her hotel room with the pretense that she had "something of extreme importance to tell him."

A few minutes after he entered

RUTH ANN STEINHAGEN
Police say she confessed

—Associated Press Wirephotos
EDDIE WAITKUS
Wounded Phillies star

Eddie Waitkus Shot In Chest With Rifle In Chicago Hotel

her room just before midnight, the girl shot him with a rifle she bought for that purpose more than a month ago.

Mr. Waitkus was shot in the right chest. The bullet punctured his lung and lodged in the back just under his heart.

Suffers Extreme Shock

Doctors at Illinois Masonic Hospital said drugs administered throughout the night were helping him overcome "extreme shock" into which he slipped after being taken to the hospital.

Hospital attendants said the wound might have meant certain death for anyone who was not in good physical condition.

They said Mr. Waitkus probably would be out of the Phillies line-up "for at least six to eight weeks and perhaps for the entire season."

Miss Steinhagen gave authorities nine statements each of which varied as to her reasons for trying to kill the ball player.

Police said she apparently was "a psychopathic personality with an urge to attract public attention through killing someone big."

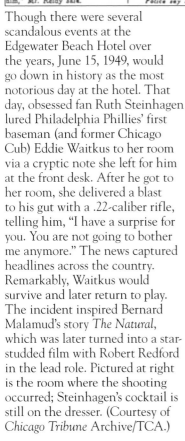

Though there were several scandalous events at the Edgewater Beach Hotel over the years, June 15, 1949, would go down in history as the most notorious day at the hotel. That day, obsessed fan Ruth Steinhagen lured Philadelphia Phillies' first baseman (and former Chicago Cub) Eddie Waitkus to her room via a cryptic note she left for him at the front desk. After he got to her room, she delivered a blast to his gut with a .22-caliber rifle, telling him, "I have a surprise for you. You are not going to bother me anymore." The news captured headlines across the country. Remarkably, Waitkus would survive and later return to play. The incident inspired Bernard Malamud's story *The Natural*, which was later turned into a star-studded film with Robert Redford in the lead role. Pictured at right is the room where the shooting occurred; Steinhagen's cocktail is still on the dresser. (Courtesy of *Chicago Tribune* Archive/TCA.)

From its earliest days, the Edgewater Beach Hotel hosted the liveliest New Year's Eve parties in Chicago, complete with ballroom dancing and a roving minstrel-like parade of musicians. For many years, these celebrations were carried on network radio. These photographs are from the 1944 party. A feature of every New Year's celebration was the crowning of a "queen" of the New Year. Miss 1944 is pictured at left bidding farewell to patrons as they leave in their coats early in the morning on the first day of the year. (Both, courtesy of *Chicago Tribune* Archive/TCA.)

Ever eager to maintain occupancy rates throughout Chicago's notorious winters, the hotel developed activities to make the hotel a destination year-round. Here, skaters prepare to hit the ice on the skating rink that was created on the hotel's tennis courts on the north side of the complex.

The late 1940s were the glory days of the beach, which natural forces had expanded by more than a dozen acres since the hotel opened in 1916. This iconic image of the hotel's beach shows how much it had grown and also how beach attire had changed in the intervening years.

The hotel tried to keep its beach off-limits to the public, but many people from the surrounding neighborhood were able to access the waters of Lake Michigan near the hotel. Pictured here is local resident Everett Stetson (center) and friends.

In this photograph, Edgewater resident George Lettner and his two children enjoy the beach near the hotel. The hotel gave the area beaches a certain cache, even for the hotel's neighbors who could not afford to stay there. (Courtesy of Marion Lettner.)

Employee recognition was a staple of William Dewey's management of the hotel. At the height of its operations, the Edgewater Beach Hotel employed more than 1,000 people. Dewey even established an employee newsletter, the *Green Shield*. One of the traditions he established was an annual dinner party held in the Marine Dining Room to honor all employees marking their 10th anniversary of service. These hardworking people who kept the hotel running on a daily basis got to appreciate the experience of the hotel's guests at least once each year.

This 1954 photograph shows hotel employees being honored for 10 years of service. The majority of them are Japanese Americans who had obtained release from World War II internment camps in order to work in the Midwest. The Edgewater Beach Hotel may have been the largest employer of Japanese Americans in the Chicago area. The descendants of many of these people still live nearby in Edgewater and other North Side Chicago neighborhoods.

William Dewey was both the general manager and an owner of the hotel, but he also took a hands-on approach to employee appreciation. He is shown here distributing thank-you gifts to employees at an annual staff recognition dinner. Among the perks was that kitchen staff who arrived early for setting up the day's menus usually received complimentary lunch in the Marine Dining Room. (Courtesy of *Chicago Tribune* Archive/TCA.)

While William Dewey worked tirelessly to maintain strong labor relations, the Edgewater Beach Hotel was not immune to the labor strife that was prevalent during the Great Depression—especially in Chicago. On August 15, 1934, a bomb ripped through the hotel's print shop, knocked out windows on several floors of the hotel, and woke 1,500 guests. The prime suspects were members of the electrical workers union who had gone on strike at the beginning of the year. (Courtesy of *Chicago Tribune* Archive/TCA.)

To manage telephone traffic, which likely exceeded that of many of the country's small towns at the time, the Edgewater Beach Hotel's switchboard handled both in-house calls and incoming and outgoing calls to the hotel. When things were extra busy, it was said that even the hotel's showgirls were pressed into doing double duty.

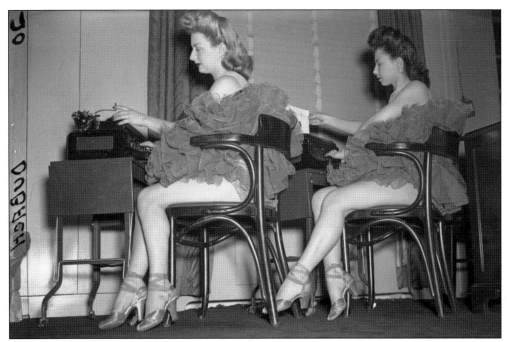

These two chorus girls are shown tending to the hotel's administrative duties between numbers. Many of the hotel's employees lived on the ninth floor of the original building, which had been turned into a dormitory. This allowed the hotel to have ready access to labor for its round-the-clock operations and saved some employees from having to commute at night to early-morning kitchen jobs. (Courtesy of *Chicago Tribune* Archive/TCA.)

Meeting the culinary demands of the hotel's guests and restaurants required an enormous kitchen operation and a small army of employees. Located on the eastern side of the original building's ground level, the kitchen could serve 3,000 meals per day with military-level precision and execution. This early photograph of the kitchen staff with Delia Trent (center) shows some of the women who made it happen. At top right is a sign that says "silence"—chatter and horseplay were strictly forbidden. (Courtesy of Delia Trent.)

This photograph of the kitchen shows staff preparing trays of banquet food in the more modern and efficient kitchen of the 1950s. George Stanton, who joined the staff in 1924 and retired as a chief executive steward in 1967, remembered, "We had 12 pastry cooks and a pastry chef and we ran it around the clock. We made everything there from dinner rolls to French bread, every kind of bread. We made all our own ice cream and sherbet." (Courtesy of Marlies Stanton.)

After being promoted to chief executive steward in 1949, George Stanton oversaw all of the hotel's catering operations, including five dining rooms with five different menus and sometimes over 1,000 meals related to convention events. In this photograph, Stanton is standing between two unidentified assistants displaying a clever version of a fish on a large tray. These unusual displays of food were a specialty of the hotel. (Courtesy of Marlies Stanton.)

Marlies Eisenaecher started her career in the hotel's kitchen. When the chief pastry chef observed her efficiency, he had her transfer to the pastry department, where she worked until the hotel closed in 1967. She met her future husband, George Stanton, in that department, and they held their 1953 wedding at the hotel. Marlies made her own elaborate wedding cake for their Marine Dining Room reception. After the hotel closed, Marlies and George purchased the very popular Swedish Bakery in the nearby Andersonville community. When they retired, it was taken over by their three children. (Courtesy of Marlies Stanton.)

Gus Travlos began working at the hotel in 1958 as chief steward of the Marine Dining Room. His uniform jacket is indicative of the professionalism the job demanded. He and his wife, June, were married at St. Andrew's Greek Orthodox Church just north of the hotel, and their wedding party was held at the Edgewater Beach Hotel. They became pillars of the Edgewater community. (Courtesy of Elaine and Tina Travlos.)

66

Four

RESIDENTIAL LIVING AT EDGEWATER BEACH

True to the vision of Benjamin Marshall, the allure of the Edgewater Beach Hotel made it a place where people of distinction would want to not only visit but also live year-round. The most direct manifestation of this vision was realized with the construction of the Edgewater Beach Apartments, which opened in October 1928.

The building containing the apartments occupied the northernmost part of the land along the shoreline, which John Corbett and John Connelly had assembled over the preceding two decades. Although the Edgewater Beach Apartments structure was not as massive as the 2,000-room Bryn Mawr Hotel originally envisioned for the site, it was nonetheless one of the largest apartment buildings of its kind in Chicago and the nation. It is the only part of the Edgewater Beach complex that remains and is still a highly sought-after address in Chicago. The Edgewater Beach Apartments opened just one year before the world plunged into the Great Depression.

Through the decades, Edgewater Beach Apartments has been home to many major figures. Bandleader Paul Whiteman, the King of Jazz, lived there while broadcasting across the nation from the hotel. Its most famous resident was George Halas, the legendary owner and coach of the Chicago Bears and one of the principal architects of the National Football League. Halas was not only a resident of the complex but also one of its owners for a time.

For eight years, the mayor of Chicago also called the Edgewater Beach Apartments home. Prominent businessman Martin Kennelly served as mayor from 1947 to 1955 before he was edged out of office by an ambitious and legendary up-and-comer named Richard J. Daley. A reformer for whom Chicago may not have been ready, Kennelly also served as mayor during one of the most fateful developments for the Edgewater Beach complex: the extension of Lake Shore Drive to Hollywood Avenue.

There were also a number of permanent residents at the hotel itself. During the depths of the Great Depression, when keeping 1,000 rooms booked was a challenge, a portion of the hotel's rooms were retrofitted with kitchenettes and other amenities that made them suitable for year-round guests.

Before plans for the hotel emerged, John Corbett and John Connery sold a handful of lots for single-family homes; one was sold in 1911 to Charles Weegham, the baseball-team owner who built what was later rechristened Wrigley Field. This photograph looks south on Sheridan Road toward the hotel in the mid-1920s and gives a flavor of the expansive lakefront houses that characterized the area. Among the noteworthy residents residing along this stretch was luncheon meat magnate Oscar Mayer. These homes did not stand long before they were demolished to make way for the expanded Edgewater Beach campus.

While Benjamin Marshall would never realize his plans to create a five-tower complex at the Edgewater Beach site, he did succeed in constructing a second tower utilizing the Maltese cross motif. The 19 stories of reinforced concrete, face brick, and terra cotta contained 307 apartments and opened in October 1928 on the site of what was originally to have been the 2,000-room Bryn Mawr hotel. The Edgewater Beach Apartments, which are now cooperative are all that remain of Marshall's grand vision. The complex still retains an extensive garden to its south and remains a highly desirable address on Chicago's north lakefront.

Construction on the Edgewater Beach Apartments started in 1926, two years after the completion of the hotel annex. Like the hotel, the building that would contain the apartments was constructed on an expedited timetable. The waterlogged site of the foundation (above) highlights the special challenges inherent in building on landfill. The top of the Edgewater Beach Apartments also featured a cupola (shown at right under construction), though of a slightly different design than those of the hotel. The large house in the foreground was later demolished to make way for additional construction. However, to this day, the area still remains a vast garden for the apartment building. Note the unusual birdhouse on the left side of the image—it is shaped like the original tower of the Edgewater Beach Hotel. Even the birds had fancy digs!

Edgewater Beach Apartments and Lake Michigan
FROM AIRPLANE - CHICAGO, ILL.

This aerial view of the Edgewater Beach Apartments illustrates the building's Maltese cross design. The tower sits atop a base that included a shopping arcade that fronted along 300 feet of Sheridan Road and a parking garage with space for 250 vehicles. This 1930s view of Chicago's lakefront shows the Edgewater Beach Apartments looming large on the shoreline.

The difficult years of the Great Depression forced management of the hotel to combat lagging occupancy rates by converting seven floors of the hotel's rooms to permanent residences in 1938. The new residential rooms at the hotel were branded the Dewey Apartments, signifying the prestige that was increasingly associated with the hotel's general manager, William Dewey. This advertisement from the *Ripples* magazine touts the advantages of living full-time in a "European" environment with direct access to restaurant dining.

AT HOME IN THE DEWEY APARTMENTS

This advertisement touting the comforts of the Dewey Apartments suggests that the target demographics for these accommodations were mature couples and single men and women. The 1940 census showed that 120 rooms at the hotel were being used by full-time residents, and 15 percent of those households also had children under the age of 18. Monthly rents ranged from $150 to $750. Among the residents were a number of major business executives, including the presidents of Pabst Blue Ribbon and the Paymaster Corporation and Thomas Lyle Williams, the founder and president of the Edgewater-based Maybelline cosmetics corporation.

This photograph of a posh model unit at the Edgewater Beach Apartments reflects the Art Deco aesthetic that was popular among the 1930s smart set. The building opened just one year before the onset of the Great Depression, which proved to be a major challenge to luxury apartment leasing for the next decade.

Like the hotel, the Edgewater Beach Apartments also offered a number of on-site amenities, including an indoor pool. Group water aerobics was among the activities offered to residents. The pool has been meticulously maintained for more than 90 years and remains active.

The Edgewater Beach Apartments were even closer to the waterfront than the hotel. This 1930s image of a wave crashing ashore just south of the apartments shows how the revetment keeps the often wild waters of Lake Michigan at bay.

Like the Edgewater Beach Hotel, the Edgewater Beach Apartments featured a shopping arcade with stores that were accessible from both the street and an interior corridor. Both buildings provided access to many of the necessities of day-to-day living, minimizing the need for guests (or residents) to leave their respective campuses. These images show two of the more popular shops at the Edgewater Beach Apartments. The Anna Held drugstore (above) had many of the essentials for day-to-day living and a soda fountain; it remains in operation. The Commissary (below) was an upscale grocer that offered gourmet foods and fine wines and also had dine-in service.

After a separation from his wife in 1939, William Dewey became a resident at the Edgewater Beach Hotel. The 1940 Census showed that Dewey was living alone at the hotel. He brought with him his two enormous Great Danes, which were well known to the staff. He continued to live at the hotel until he retired as general manager in 1952. Dewey did not have a long retirement, as he died two years after relinquishing the job he held for 36 years.

Undoubtedly, the most famous resident of the apartments was the legendary George Halas, owner and head coach of the Chicago Bears and a key architect of the National Football League. Halas, shown here in front of the apartments with his wife, Minnie, was a resident for 39 years. George was among the investor group of residents who bought the building in 1949. When he died in 1983, his funeral was held at nearby St. Ita's Catholic Church. He held many celebrations at the hotel over the years, including a number of raucous Chicago Bears reunions.

For eight years, none other than the mayor of Chicago called the Edgewater Beach Apartments home. Martin Kennelly, already a wealthy businessman, was elected as a reform candidate in 1947 to clean up city government. He served two terms before being edged aside by an ambitious county clerk named Richard J. Daley, whose old-style brand of machine politics seemed to better suit local ward bosses. The first year Kennelly was in office, the city approved plans to extend Lake Shore Drive northward by more than a half mile. (Courtesy of the University of Illinois at Chicago Richard J. Daley Library.)

Among the children who grew up at the Edgewater Beach Hotel was Marilou Hedlund, who would later become one of the first two women elected to the Chicago City Council in 1971. In a 1989 interview with the *Chicago Reader*, Hedlund recounted her childhood at the hotel that was filled with misadventures involving hotel staff and various circus animals, like elephants, camels, and even a seal that was housed in a tank in the parking garage and that Hedlund was allowed to feed. She was also starstruck by encounters with Hollywood celebrities, such as Barbara Stanwyck. Hedlund's life inspired the series of *Eloise* books.

For his snowbird clients, Benjamin Marshall created another luxury hotel experience 800 miles south of Chicago in Biloxi, Mississippi. The Edgewater Gulf Hotel was a stunning 400-room Art Deco structure designed by Marshall and Fox to offer the same amenities guests had come to expect in Chicago. Opened in 1926, the Edgewater Gulf was one of the largest hotels on the gulf in its day and was also managed by Dewey. It had a much more extensive campus, including an 18-hole golf course. In the era before air travel, the hotel's location was readily accessible to Chicagoans via the Illinois Central Railroad.

Much like at the Edgewater Beach Hotel, one of the prime gathering spots at the Edgewater Gulf was a great room dominated by a four-sided hearth, though this one was executed in the Art Deco style of the rest of the hotel.

Five

A NATIONALLY RENOWNED MUSICAL MECCA

From the Edgewater Beach Hotel's earliest days, music was central to its identity and appeal. The hotel had two legendary venues for music: the Marine Dining Room and the Beach Walk. By the early 1920s, the Edgewater Beach Hotel had gained such fame that budding jazz legend Bix Beiderbecke abruptly abandoned his academic career, explaining to his parents that he "had a chance to make a few bucks at the Edgewater Beach Hotel."

Many of the most acclaimed jazz orchestras of the 1920s and 1930s routinely played the Edgewater Beach Hotel, and some of them made their names there. Paul Whiteman, Tommy Dorsey, and Xavier Cugat were all regulars. A young Lawrence Welk played some of his earliest gigs there. In later years, legends like Tony Bennett performed. Supplementing the music was a lively dance scene, as hundreds of couples at a time would crowd onto the dance floors of the Marine Dining Room and the Beach Walk—the only outdoor marble dance floor in the nation.

Much of this music was enjoyed not just by hotel patrons but also by radio audiences across the Midwest. The hotel was a seminal site for live radio music in the 1920s and had its own radio station, WEBH, constructed in a room just off the main lobby and adjacent to the Marine Dining Room. The station's broadcasts became one of the hotel's most effective advertising channels and gave rise to its international reputation. WEBH was set up by two inventive young tinkerers who later founded the Zenith Radio Company.

Often accompanying the music were lively floor shows featuring bevies of dancing girls under the iron-fisted direction of two choreographers who later went on to achieve major success in other venues.

THE LAST WALTZ WITH YOU WAS
The SWEETEST WALTZ of ALL

Featured By
Dan Russo & Ted Fiorito's
Oriole Orchestra
Edgewater Beach Hotel, Chicago

Words & Music
by
CHARLES HARRISON
and
FRED ROSE

Ted Browne Music
218 SOUTH WABASH A
Chicago

For years, the Edgewater Beach Hotel had one of the best house orchestras in the nation. While the leaders of the bands changed over the years, the quality of the musical offerings never flagged. Dan Russo, a violinist, and, Ted Fio-Rito, a keyboardist, formed the Oriole Orchestra, the hotel's second house orchestra. The Oriole Orchestra was the lead band at the Edgewater Beach Hotel for four years before Russo struck out on his own in 1927.

Harry Sosnik, who directed many orchestras over his long career, was a regular at the Edgewater Beach Hotel in its early years. Decades later, when television became America's top source for entertainment, Sosnik became a household name as the music director for *Your Hit Parade*.

HARRY SOSNIK AND HIS ORCHESTRA
EDGEWATER BEACH HOTEL
CHICAGO

MARK FISHER'S EDGEWATER BEACH HOTEL ORCHESTRA

One of the more popular orchestras at the Beach Walk was Mark Fisher's. Though he never became a household name, Fisher did write one of the most enduring songs of the American songbook, "When You're Smiling," which has been covered by everyone from Louis Armstrong to Michael Bublé.

The fame of the music scene at the Marine Dining Room was such that in January 1922, when 19-year-old Leon "Bix" Beiderbecke got wind of an opportunity to join a combo playing there, the soon-to-be-legendary cornet player jettisoned his academic career at Lake Forest Academy to join a jazz band of Northwestern students playing at a prom for Edgewater's Senn High School. Beiderbecke explained to his long-suffering Iowa parents, "You see, I have the chance to play the Edgewater Beach Hotel and make some dough."

The opening of the Beach Walk season was a major event at the Edgewater Beach Hotel and always featured a major lineup of talent reminiscent of an early television variety program, including singers and even animal acts. In addition to headliner Wayne King, the opening program for 1945 featured the singing group the Stylists, Gaudsmiths's Dogs, and hotel organist Betty Gray.

Proclaimed the King of Jazz, Paul Whiteman was an irrepressible composer, conductor, and bandleader as well as a violinist. He was one of the top figures in jazz and had a seven-month residency at the Edgewater Beach Hotel in 1931. Among his career highlights was leading the orchestra for the premiere of Gershwin's *Rhapsody in Blue*. Whiteman lived on the 17th floor of the Edgewater Beach Apartments during his stay. Whiteman died in 1967 during the same week the Edgewater Beach closed. Acclaimed composer and arranger Ferde Grofe worked with Whiteman for several months at the hotel.

Ted Fio-Rito was a regular bandleader at the hotel throughout the 1920s. It was during this time that he wrote his most famous song, "Toot Toot Tootsie Goodbye," which would become an unofficial anthem of the Roaring Twenties. While at the hotel, Fio-Rito recorded more than 100 songs for the Decca, Columbia, and Victor record labels.

Appearing with Ted Fio-Rito's band in 1922 was a 13-year-old musical prodigy named Benny Goodman. The clarinetist, who hailed from Chicago's West Side Jewish community, was later dubbed the King of Swing and became one of the most popular figures in jazz music.

Latin jazz great Xavier Cugat was a regular at the Edgewater Beach Hotel for more than 20 years. Cugat, shown here with singer Abbe Lane, created one of the most talked-about incidents in hotel history when his wife stormed into his room and discovered that he and Lane had something more than a professional relationship. Lane ended up becoming the fourth Mrs. Cugat in 1952. They recorded together on the Mercury label in 1961. Among his many achievements, Cugat gave Desi Arnaz his professional start playing the congas in his orchestra at the hotel.

ORRIN TUCKER'S ORCHESTRA
and GLEE CLUB *with* HARRIETT SMITH'S LOVELY LADIES
MARINE ROOM - EDGEWATER BEACH HOTEL, CHICAGO

Orrin Tucker played the alto sax and led his first band in Naperville, Illinois. He went on to become a major recording artist, and his most famous song was "Oh Johnny, How You Can Love" in 1939. He made over 100 recordings for Columbia Records between 1938 and 1942.

Russ Morgan was another well-known performer who played the hotel. An accomplished trombonist and piano player, Morgan also wrote the hit 1939 song "You're Nobody 'Til Somebody Loves You," which later became a staple in the repertoires of both Dean Martin and Frank Sinatra.

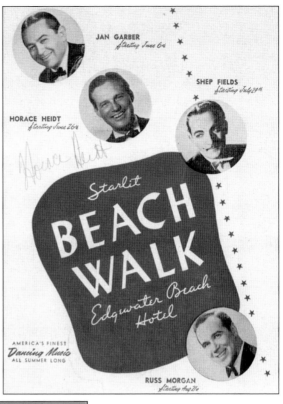

Another popular bandleader was Wayne King from Savanna, Illinois, who played alto sax. King started with the Paul Whiteman Orchestra in 1924 before breaking out on his own. King joined the Army in 1940, but he returned after the war in 1945 to again lead his orchestra at the hotel.

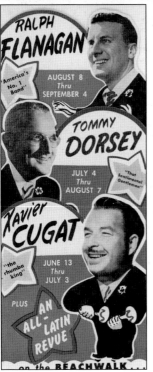

Long before he launched his television variety show, Lawrence Welk began to establish his fame at the Edgewater Beach Hotel and then moved on to become a long-running act at Chicago's Aragon and Trianon ballrooms. Welk was another bandleader who employed a young Desi Arnaz at the hotel. This 1939 photograph, with Mildred Stanley holding a sign urging the United States to exercise geopolitical neutrality, reflects the divided sentiments at the time about involvement in another war in Europe. Note the Marine Dining Room bandstand, which was used for years. (Courtesy of *Chicago Tribune* Archive/TCA.)

The Dorsey Brothers, Tommy and Jimmy, were well-known at the hotel, but Jimmy spent more time there. He was a jazz clarinetist, saxophonist, and composer who performed at the Edgewater Beach Hotel in 1950 and 1951. His last hit was "So Rare," released in 1957.

Bandleader and tenor saxophonist Freddy Martin (right) gained fame for his jazzy adaptations of classical works by Rachmaninoff, Grieg, and others. He also had a good ear for up-and-coming singers. Future television talk and game show impresario Merv Griffin was among those who sang with Martin's orchestra at the Edgewater Beach Hotel. Martin's orchestra made appearances in 1952 and 1954.

A NIGHT SCENE OF EDGEWATER BEACH HOTEL FROM LAKE MICHIGAN —CHICAGO

The Edgewater Beach Hotel might have been at its most glamorous at night. Even if one could not get into the Beach Walk, they could still hear the music drifting across the water along the lakefront. The hotel exuded a sense of romance for many. Bandleader Romeo Meltz recalled, "I worked at the Beach Walk for a summer. I met my wife there. I dated her and eventually married her. I'm building this up for you because the story of the Edgewater Beach Hotel is really the story of my life."

Napoleon Gray

Napoleon Gray Dance Floor, Edgewater Beach Hotel, Chicago, Illinois

A Marble Dance Floor

So far as we know, this is the only outside marble dance floor in the country.

In 1920 The Edgewater Beach Hotel, on Lake Michigan, Chicago, decided to build an uncovered dance floor directly on the beach, a few feet from the water.

As it would be subject to summer rains as well as winter snows, it necessarily had to be of some material not affected by the elements. Napoleon Gray Marble in tiles 8 inches by 16 inches was the choice.

The floor has stood up so well that lately another section has been added.

PHENIX MARBLE COMPANY

KANSAS CITY   MISSOURI

The Beach Walk's dance floor was covered in Napoleon Gray marble and thought to be the only outdoor marble dance floor in the nation. As a very durable material, it stood up to Chicago's often snowy winters and blistering summers as well as the dancing feet of countless revelers over the decades. The 5,000-square-foot dance floor was crowned with a classic band shell at its far end.

The Beach Walk dance floor was the place to be on a summer night. Often, it seemed everyone was there at the same time. Only drinks were served, and they could only be ordered when the band took a break. This 1948 photograph shows how close the dance floor was to the lake. One was lucky to get a table.

This 1948 scene on the Beach Walk dance
floor was included in a Fox-Movietone newsreel
on Chicago, with the Edgewater Beach Hotel
illustrating the epitome of Chicago's lively and
elegant nightlife scene. Despite cool August
weather on the night of the filming, the game
audience stayed late into the evening to make
sure the filmmakers got what they needed.
Edgewater resident Bill Birch is the man behind
the camera; he would go on to have a long
career in the movie and television business.

Service on the Beach Walk was fast and efficient.
Romeo Meltz, a bandleader who also tended bar,
recalled this: "When the Beach Walk opened in
the summer, I was promoted to bartender. That's
when the big bands were playing on the Beach
Walk and people would be dancing. And then,
when the set was over, all the waiters would come
over because everyone wanted to be served at the
same time. So we had to set up the drinks before.
Like we had trays and trays and trays of scotch
and bourbon poured, fixings for mint juleps."

Fowler and Tamara and their Seven-Piece Marimba Band will be presented on the Beach Walk this Season, commencing on the occasion of the Formal Opening, Saturday Evening, June 16.

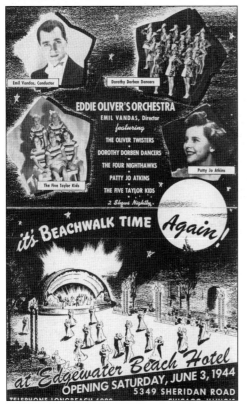

Ballroom dancing was often a part of floor shows at the hotel. The team of Fowler and Tamara were among the most popular dance acts of the era and were noted for their tango dancing, exotic costumes, and guitar music. They appeared at the Marine Dining Room in 1925 before touring around the country.

The Dorothy Dorben Dancers began performing at the Edgewater Beach Hotel in the early 1930s with many exotic performances. Their routines typically were the culmination of nightly floor shows starting at 8:40 p.m. and 11:30 p.m. Dorben was praised in the Chicago media for the creativity of her shows, especially a 1943 program titled *The Surrey with the Fringe on Top*, which used music from the hit show *Oklahoma!* Dorben later took her shows to a number of other Chicago hotels.

The Dorothy Hild Dancers, who replaced the Dorothy Dorben Dancers, were also regular performers at floor shows in the Marine Dining Room. These were widely lauded in the Chicago media and often included other performers, including puppeteers, acrobats, and stilt walkers. Here, performers present a fan dance number reminiscent of the iconic performer Sally Rand. Frequently, these floor shows also had themes, including Ancient Egypt, the Arabian Nights, Paper Dolls, and the Spangled Bolero. (Courtesy of the Dorothy Hild Papers, Newberry Library, Chicago.)

This publicity still of the Dorothy Hild Dancers shows them in costumes that created the illusion of more skin than they were actually revealing. Their popularity at the Edgewater Beach Hotel led to engagements at other hotels around Chicago.

This publicity photo highlights the youth and beauty of the Dorothy Hild Dancers. One dancer was Barbara Ferverde, who took the stage name Barbara Bouche (second row, far right) and first auditioned in the early 1940s. She had been a dance instructor, but after a divorce, she took a chance on the big city and landed a job with Dorothy Hild. Her roommate was Mary Lou Hai (third row, far right), a young Japanese American woman who had been in an internment camp before working at the Edgewater Beach Hotel. (Courtesy of Roberta Estes.)

Barbara Bouche, shown here in a publicity photo, later reported how strenuous it was being a member of the Dorothy Hild and how she would shed pounds during each performance. Every four months, a series of four new shows was created, and new routines would have to be learned. (Courtesy of Roberta Estes.)

A seemingly endless menagerie of exotic animals would routinely grace the performances in the Marine Dining Room. Here, Dorothy Hild is running through the paces on the beach with a camel for an upcoming performance with an Arabesque theme. (Courtesy of the Dorothy Hild Papers, Newberry Library, Chicago.)

Throughout the 1950s and into the 1960s, numerous top performers continued to play at the Edgewater Beach Hotel even after the era of big band music started to fall by the wayside. Among the major singing stars to grace the stages during this era was crooner Tony Bennett, who performed at the hotel early in his career that spanned more than 70 years.

Legendary jazz singer Sarah Vaughan was another entertainer who performed at the Marine Dining Room, appearing in 1963. Other major performers who came through in later years included bandleader Woody Herman, singer Patti Page, and teenage heartthrob Frankie Avalon, whose appearance during the hotel's final year caused a minor riot among fans.

The Edgewater Beach Hotel played a key role in the advent of commercial radio. It launched the careers of two young entrepreneurs who would go on to establish the Zenith Radio Corporation. Under the leadership of manager William M. Dewey, the hotel operated its own radio station, WEBH. Dewey was among the first businessmen to grasp the impact that the young medium of radio could have in brand-building for businesses. For decades to come, but especially in the Roaring Twenties, the hotel was synonymous with jazz music broadcasts from the Marine Dining Room.

In 1919, Edgewater Beach Hotel general manager William Dewey allowed two young World War I veterans—Ralph H.G. Mathews and Karl E. Hassel—to build a small "radio shack" on vacant hotel property. The building housed their radio receiver manufacturing business (relocated from Mathews's parents' home) and equipment for radio station 9ZN, for which Mathews had received the license while he was a student at Lane Technical High School. The station's antennas were two windmill towers. From this tiny operation grew the Zenith Radio Corporation, which would become the largest producer of radios in America and an early television manufacturer.

In 1922, Ralph H.G. Mathews and Karl E. Hassel received a commercial radio license for a station that would bear the call letters WJAZ. Eager to further integrate the world of radio into the identity of the hotel, in 1923, general manager William Dewey partnered with the two entrepreneurs and constructed a state-of-the-art broadcasting booth— the Crystal Studio— that overlooked the Marine Dining Room.

Transmitter

In 1923, the radio station's transmitter was in a small building 300 feet north of the hotel. In 1927, the recently created Federal Radio Commission forced WEBH to share time on a new frequency with the more powerful KYW, which was not favorable to either party. Dewey accepted KYW's buyout, and WEBH went off the air on June 30, 1928. But the era of broadcasting from the Edgewater Beach Hotel was not over. It had established its musical brand, and courtesy of NBC, the hotel was wired for remote transmission of live music and continued to broadcast music for decades to come.

The radio station studio's glass walls made it possible for audiences to participate in the excitement of this new medium, as shown in this 1923 photograph taken from outside the Crystal Studio. In April 1958, WEBH was reborn as an FM station thanks to former disk jockey Buddy Black. It played easy listening and jazz-influenced popular songs on weekdays and light classical music on weekends. A distinctive feature of the station was that announcers read news reports over soft background music. It broadcasted until the hotel's final day in December 1967.

In 1924, general manager William Dewey hired station manager Robert Boniel, who initiated remote hookups of live music and coined a new slogan: "Voice of Middle West." On a shoestring budget, Boniel expanded the programming of the station, including the launch of an annual New Year's Eve broadcast that endured for decades.

Robert Boniel gave the first radio gig to two comedians, Freeman Gosden and Charles Correll. They quickly parlayed their success at into a long-term lucrative contract with WGN Radio, where they became the first performers to produce a weekly serialized radio program. That program eventually morphed into *Amos 'n' Andy,* the nation's most popular radio program in the 1930s and 1940s and later a major flashpoint over the representation of African Americans in popular culture.

The cavalcade of orchestras playing at the hotel through the 1920s cemented its reputation as a musical mecca across much of the nation. Pictured here are Ted Fio-Rito and his Oriole Orchestra playing on the Marine Dining Room's elevated bandstand. The window between the bandstand and the control room (visible in the middle of this photograph) allowed the announcer/control panel operator to cue the bandleader when it was time to play.

STATION W-G-N

CHICAGO TRIBUNE, Zenith Station, Begins Broadcasting at 6 o'clock tonight from the Edgewater Beach Hotel. Wave Length 370 meters.

INAUGURAL PROGRAM 6 p. m Saturday to 8 a. m. Sunday

The Chicago Tribune intends to maintain in its broadcasting standards of entertainment and instruction worthy of the call letters WGN. Watch The Tribune every day for detailed programs.

The Chicago Tribune
THE WORLD'S GREATEST NEWSPAPER

Popular station WGN had important early ties to the Edgewater Beach Hotel. On March 29, 1924, WGN first took to the airwaves—but not from its own studio, which was still under construction. It aired from Crystal Studio, which Edgewater Beach Hotel general manager William Dewey leased to the *Chicago Tribune*–owned WGN along with the hotel's radio signal. WGN's inaugural broadcast included an overnight extravaganza of music and spoken-word programming. Dewey and Mayor William Dever were guests as well. WGN broadcasted from the hotel for two months. Once WGN departed, Dewey resumed control of the station and purchased the interests of the Zenith partners.

Six

A Unique Theater on the Lake

Over the past half-century, Chicago has gained a reputation for its gritty, grassroots "storefront" theater scene. But before this theatrical renaissance of the 1970s and later, Chicago had some other interesting chapters in local theater, two of which were centered on the Edgewater Beach Hotel.

During its early years, the Edgewater Beach Hotel hosted a variety of productions that literally took place right on the water. In what might have been a one-of-a-kind undertaking, a stage was constructed on a pier that projected into Lake Michigan. Audiences were seated along the Beach Walk at tables set along the shore and also on the steps of the revetment leading down to the water.

Later, in the 1950s, after the hotel lost its direct access to the waterfront, another unique theater scene arose. Started by impresario Marshall Migatz and later managed by Noel Behn, a summer stock theater was created on the marble dance floor under a big-top tent more typically employed for trapeze artists and elephant acts rather than Broadway stars. During its seven years in operation, the theater drew some of the biggest names in show business—including legendary performers such as Mae West, Groucho Marx, and Tallulah Bankhead—for a variety of productions ranging from classics and dramas to light comedies and even avant-garde theater of the absurd.

One of the more unusual features of the Edgewater Beach Hotel was its theater on the lake. Constructed on a pier just east of the Marine Dining Room, the lake stage appeared to be floating on the water. In front of the stage is the orchestra pit. A small backstage area was concealed by the backdrop scenery. Actors had to project mightily to be heard over the breaking waves.

Though most of the shows presented at the Edgewater Beach's most unusual theater tended toward light opera, it also took on weightier productions. This scene is from a staging of Charles Gonoud's fire-and-brimstone-filled *Faust*. It is unclear how many seasons the Edgewater Beach's novel theater-on-the-lake scene endured.

The cast of *Faust* is shown making a dramatic arrival to the stage via gondola in this publicity still. Creating a sense of the dramatic became an enduring facet in William Dewey's management of the hotel.

Audiences for the theater on the lake were seated at cabaret tables arrayed along the Beach Walk. The cheap seats were along the revetment wall.

Long before Chicago became world-famous for its gritty "storefront" theater scene in the 1970s, the Edgewater Beach Playhouse was one of a handful of venues on Chicago's North Side presenting theater in the 1950s and 1960s. Though it was just a seasonal playhouse, it attracted major stars to its productions. After Lake Shore Drive was extended, the Beach Walk lost its allure for music and dancing. Its space was used for a summer theater launched in 1955 by Marshall Migatz, who produced just one season that included shows starring Uta Hagan and Eva Gabor. Fortunately, another budding impresario was ready to take over—Noel Behn, who later became a major Hollywood writer, notably for the television show *Homicide*. In 1957, under Behn, a new summer theater was dedicated in an enormous tent that accommodated up to 950 patrons. The theater hosted productions featuring scores of stars over the next six seasons. From the start, productions were challenged due to being staged in a tent, which was initially open-sided. Lakefront breezes and other weather factors sometimes forced relocation into the Marine Dining Room. Still, major actors, including Burgess Meredith, Steve Allen, and Eve Arden, performed there.

The 1959 season was especially noteworthy, including a rare late-career appearance by Groucho Marx, who starred in a play he cowrote titled *Time for Elizabeth*. Marx was at the height of his fame at the time due to his popular television quiz show program *You Bet Your Life*. Hollywood leading man Franchot Tone and Method actress Susan Strasbourg starred in George Bernard Shaw's *Caesar and Cleopatra*. In that same season, Chicago native and Oscar-winner Dorothy Malone appeared with her husband, Jacques Bergerac, in *Once More with Feeling*.

Many stars were brought in for the 1960 season. Tony Randall appeared for a two-week run in the play *Good Bye Again* a decade before he achieved enduring fame as neat freak Felix Unger in the television sitcom version of Neil Simon's hit *The Odd Couple*.

STAGEBILL
Chicago's Theatre Magazine

TALLULAH BANKHEAD
"Craig's Wife"
EDGEWATER BEACH PLAYHOUSE

One of America's most flamboyant actresses, Tallulah Bankhead appeared in the 1960 drama *Craig's Wife*. Other performers who appeared at the hotel that year were Chicago-born late-night talk-show pioneer Steve Allen and his wife, Jayne Meadows, in the comedy *The Four Poster Bed*.

EDGEWATER BEACH PLAYHOUSE

STAGEBILL
Chicago's Theatre Magazine

Miss MAE WEST
in "SEXTETTE"

This 1961 playbill is from the opening night of legendary Hollywood sex siren Mae West's signature show *Sextette*. Fifteen years later, West, then in her mid-80s, would star in a film adaptation of the play, capping her long career. West's costar in the Edgewater Beach production was veteran Hollywood actor Alan Marshal. Sadly, the 52-year-old Marshal was found dead (of heart failure) in his room at the hotel on July 13, 1961.

One of the more unusual shows staged at the Edgewater Beach Playhouse was *Rhinoceros*, Eugene Ionescu's avant-garde absurdist takedown of life under totalitarianism. Coming directly from Broadway with star Zero Mostel, the Chicago production also starred Ralph Meeker, who stepped into the role at the last minute when Milton Berle could not agree on terms. In one performance, Mostel recalled, he had to get on his hands and knees so that the microphones embedded along the stage lights would pick up his voice over the noise of a driving rainstorm.

Fresh off her 1962 Oscar win for *West Side Story*, actress Rita Moreno starred in Christopher Isherwood's *I Am a Camera*. The show was an earlier production of the story that was later adapted into *Cabaret*.

OSSIE DAVIS   RUBY DEE
in
"PURLIE VICTORIOUS"

Ossie Davis and Ruby Dee were the first couple of African American theater and had one of their greatest successes with *Purlie Victorious*, a comedy set in the Jim Crow South. It played at the Edgewater Beach Playhouse before later opening on Broadway, where it garnered numerous Tony Awards and other accolades. In 1963, it was turned into the film *Gone Are the Days*.

Undoubtedly, much of the motivation for keeping the theater going was to build traffic for the hotel's restaurants. This advertisement illustrates the efforts to build synergy between the two. By the end of the 1961 theater season, the hotel had decided to stake its future on the convention trade, which made theater at the hotel expendable.

Seven

KEEPING PACE WITH CHANGING TIMES

Throughout World War II and its aftermath, the Edgewater Beach Hotel remained a major destination for vacationers, conventioneers, and thrill-seekers. But it was not immune to the major social changes that came to the United States in the wake of the war. Much of the middle class that had defined the country's big cities began decamping to the suburbs, leaving the Edgewater Beach complex distanced from much of its key audience. Perhaps more important was the growing prevalence of automobile ownership in America and shifting tastes for vacationers to "hit the road" rather than taking their holidays locally.

The most visible manifestation of the changing landscape of the hotel was the extension of Lake Shore Drive, which was completed by the mid-1950s and cut off the complex from its namesake waterfront. Hotel management responded by constructing an Olympic-sized swimming pool and cabana complex, which itself became host to a lively social scene over the next decade.

Perhaps the most significant—but least visible—change at the hotel came about in 1948 with its sale to the Hotel Corporation of America, a chain of six hotels that included New York City's famed Roosevelt Hotel. After that sale, general manager William Dewey was no longer an owner. He relinquished his role as general manager in 1952, but his retirement was brief, as he died in 1954. It is possible that the hotel never again had quite the same level of service as a result.

With Chicago's postwar emergence as the convention capital of America, the hotel made a push to become a major player in the trade and executed large-scale renovations that stripped the hotel of much of its original charm in the early 1960s. Though the hotel could boast of being the closest convention hotel to Chicago's O'Hare International Airport, it found itself too far away from the convention center of gravity in Chicago's Loop and closer to the new McCormick Place Convention Center, the largest in the world.

One national organization that did routinely bring its meeting business to the hotel in the 1960s was the International Brotherhood of Teamsters and its controversial leader, Jimmy Hoffa. He conducted much of the organization's business from a $1,000-a-day suite just as federal prosecutors were closing in on his alleged misdeeds. This—and other associations—started to give the complex a slightly "mobbed-up" reputation, which reportedly did not please Chicago's all-powerful mayor Richard J. Daley.

These two photographs show how the beach in front of the hotel grew in a relatively short amount of time. The above image is from the mid-1930s and shows construction still underway on the parkland lakefill south of Foster Avenue. A small beach is visible in front of the hotel. The below image, from the late 1940s, shows a considerable expansion of the beach that was caused by the natural flow of water and sand.

Throughout the 1930s and 1940s, Lake Shore Drive became a major traffic artery between downtown Chicago and its wealthy North Shore suburbs. When it terminated just south of the hotel, heavy highway-level traffic was dumped onto Sheridan Road, as shown in this 1952 photograph. Traffic was often backed up for miles. An extension of Lake Shore Drive past the hotel seemed inevitable.

Chicago approved the extension of Lake Shore Drive to Hollywood Avenue in 1947, the year Edgewater Beach Apartment resident Martin Kennelly became mayor. This meant landfilling the lake east of the hotel and cutting off the direct waterfront access of the hotel and the apartments. This image shows how the hotel (in the upper left corner) became landlocked as a result.

Steel plates were driven into the lakebed about 500 feet east of the hotel, establishing where the new shoreline would be. Hotel guests were treated to a show of a giant "sand sucker" machine vacuuming up waterlogged sand and redepositing it into the lake. This landfilling is still underway on the far left in this image. Solid earth excavated from the construction of Chicago's Eisenhower Expressway was used for the new lakefill. The pointer at the top of the image shows the roadbed taking shape just north of Foster Avenue.

The Lake Shore Drive extension to Bryn Mawr was opened in 1956 with a ceremony. The drive's final extension to Hollywood Avenue was completed the following year. Chicago's lakefront is almost 100 percent man-made, and roughly five square miles of the city were created on lake landfill. A total of 55 acres of additional landfill were added as part of the Lake Shore Drive extension. The concrete structure at lower left is the Bryn Mawr Avenue underpass.

This image shows the expansion of Lincoln Park east of Lake Shore Drive, which was part of the extension. The new beach at Foster could still be accessed from the hotel via the pedestrian footpath visible just east of the hotel. But it was a far cry from having the beach just outside the hotel's back door. After the loss of beach access, hotel managers installed an Olympic-sized pool, which opened in 1953, allowing guests to enjoy continued outdoor summer fun. Constructed north of the original hotel building, the pool replaced the golf course. As the largest private pool in the city, it was a focal point for summer activities, including swim meets and fashion shows, for the next 15 years. Alas, this was not able to halt the slide in business over the next decade. In 1954, the hotel added a two-story complex of private cabanas around the pool.

MAESTRO JOHNNY PINEAPPLE and his Aloha Maids, Leilani (left) and Kealoha, enjoy pool-side cut-ups at the Edgewater Beach Hotel's Pool and Cabana Club. The trio, with the Pineapple orchestra, appear Wednesday through Sunday in the Edgewater's exotic Polynesian Village, popular successor to the once famed Marine Dining Room

The pool hosted numerous social events and programs over the 15 years it existed. Not only did it provide opportunities for swimming and diving events, but there were also beauty contests, fashion shows, and other activities that generated publicity for the hotel. Even Johnny Weissmuller returned for an encore appearance some 40 years after beginning his climb to fame at the hotel. This issue of the hotel's magazine shows how the South Seas vibe of the hotel's new Polynesian Room was also available poolside, where a luau atmosphere often prevailed in the summertime.

Throughout the 1950s and 1960s, many major events took place at the Edgewater Beach Hotel. Civil rights leader Martin Luther King Jr. spoke at the 1963 National Conference on Religion and Race at the hotel. His speech, titled "A Challenge to Justice and Love," was given on January 16 to commemorate the 100th anniversary of the Emancipation Proclamation.

These two 1950s advertisements show how the hotel was working to develop patronage among local residents in an effort to promote the concept of what would later be called the "staycation." The advertisement at right touts the hotel's amenities and waterfront location and (perhaps overly eagerly?) compares a weekend at the Edgewater Beach Hotel to a visit to the Riviera. The advertisement below promotes the hotel as a family-friendly destination at a time when millions of American families were packing up for road trips.

What!
A
Riviera
in Chicago?

Of course! It's the incomparable Edgewater Beach Hotel . . . the ideal setting for a Riviera Week End in Chicago

Magnificent outdoor pool—Tennis—Five famous restaurants—with dining, dancing and floor show nightly in the exotic Polynesian Village. Summer Theatre right on the grounds. Smart shops. Ample in-hotel parking . . , and just 18 minutes from the Loop.

Plan now for an exciting RIVIERA Week End . . . Week . . or an evening at the Edgewater Beach. All outside rooms with a beautiful view. . . . rates start at $9 per person, per day (double occupancy) and there's no charge for children under 14 in your room (Special attraction: Experienced baby sitters available).

· Phone LOngbeach 1-6000
for reservations.

5300 North Sheridan Road,
Chicago 40, Illinois

Edward L. Buckley V.P. & General Manager
AN HCA HOTEL
The "Riviera" of Chicago

at the Edgewater Beach in Chicago

plan a carefree family week-end close to home

Here's the way you can have an extra *family* vacation this summer . . . only a short drive from your home, you can enjoy the famous "country club" atmosphere of the Edgewater Beach Hotel.

Relax with the youngsters in the outdoor pool, on the tennis courts. Enjoy the lake and its breezes which cool our acres of shaded lawns.

Treat them to the finest of food in any of five exciting dining spots (No dishes to wash, either!). And, at night there's dancing under the stars or a summer theatre (right at the Hotel near the children) for you and the Mrs.

There's NO ROOM CHARGE for the under-14-year-olds in your room on Friday, Saturday, and Sunday, and naturally, there's no charge for swimming or tennis.

Write for a free booklet "Exciting Adventures in Chicago" . . . or better yet, make your reservations now.

FOR A NIGHT OF TROPICAL SPLENDOR

in the moonlit compound of a native Polynesian Village—and around you a combination of all the exotic idylls of the Far Pacific—of Michener, of Joseph Conrad, of Stevenson and Captain Cook. Here is a hut from Sumatra; over there a facade from the Indonesian Archipelago, while, beyond, the green sea of jungle foliage stirs softly in the blossom-scented night winds. In every direction your eye encounters one exotic vista after another—from Bali, Surabaja, Java, Bora

Bora, Tahiti and all the other romantic lands beyond the sea. Then on your tables, hand-hewn out of Hawaiian Monkey-Pod Trees which were ancient even before Waikiki knew the first footprint of the white man, you will enjoy the sensual delights of an epicurean experience in authentic Polynesian foods and tropical drinks. This, indeed, is Paradise Unspoiled...as lived and loved by the people of the Islands—and those of you who come to dine and dance in the...

Polynesian Village

AIR CONDITIONED

After the addition of the pool, perhaps the most dramatic change at the hotel in the 1950s was the 1955 conversion of the Marine Dining Room into the Polynesian Village, an over-the-top rendering of a South Pacific island village. The rage for such fare, which also spurred Trader Vic's,

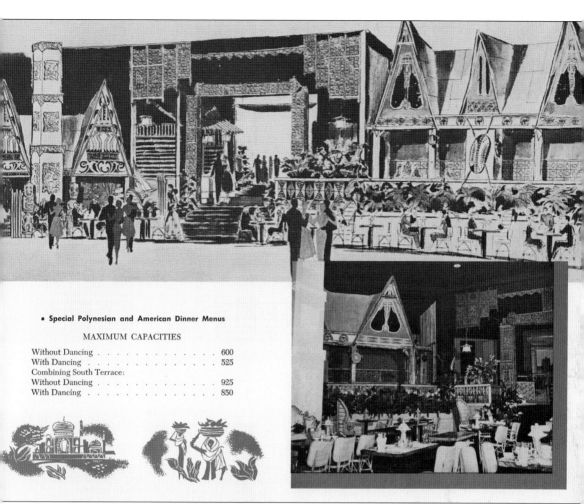

- **Special Polynesian and American Dinner Menus**

MAXIMUM CAPACITIES

Without Dancing	600
With Dancing	525
Combining South Terrace:	
Without Dancing	925
With Dancing	850

Kon Tiki Ports, and a number of other similarly themed restaurants around the country, was at its height in the 1950s, when it took advantage of the cultural impact of returning World War II vets and the musical *South Pacific*.

The creation of Polynesian Village also necessitated a whole new genre of musical entertainment. This poster touts Hawaiian performer Gene Rains and his band, which provided a relaxing musical sound with vibraphones and ukuleles.

By the late 1950s, business was decidedly down at the hotel. The advent of car travel and commercial airline service gave many Americans more leisure and vacation options. Hotel management responded by refocusing the hotel on business meetings and conventions. They spent nearly $1 million remodeling the hotel, stripping away much of its vintage charm in the process and giving it a more streamlined look. They also spent heavily on air-conditioning, and had artificially cooled about 70 percent of the hotel by 1961.

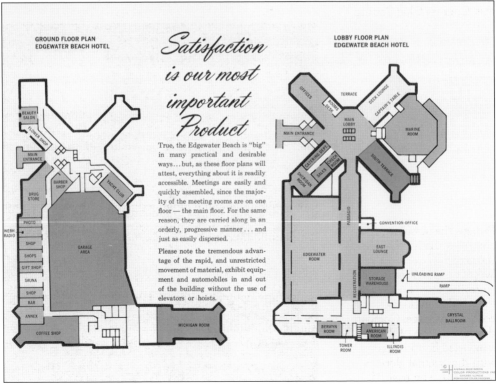

The retrofitting of the Edgewater Beach Hotel for the convention trade dramatically remade the look and feel of the hotel. What had been the romantic Marine Dining Room—and later, the exotic Polynesian Village—was remade into a buttoned-down, corporate-style event space. The hotel's marketing brochures promised convention planners that "meetings benefit from the lack of downtown distractions, traffic noises and general big city confusion, assuring you of higher attendance at all your sessions. And, when the day's deliberations are done, there's nothing like this 'Country Club Setting.'"

Perhaps the most jarring change at the hotel was in the graceful old East and West Lounges, which were basically gutted and retrofitted to provide additional convention space. Compare this photograph of the banal remodeled East Lounge with the original glorious lounge space on page 35.

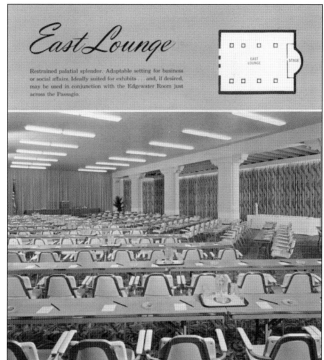

East Lounge

Restrained palatial splendor. Adaptable setting for business or social affairs. Ideally suited for exhibits . . . and, if desired, may be used in conjunction with the Edgewater Room just across the Passagio.

This advertisement reflects the hotel's effort to attract business travelers with its business-by-day and country-club-at-night appeal. The hotel also made a play to capture its share of America's booming convention business, which Chicago dominated for the first four decades after World War II. A hotel executive told the *Chicago Tribune* in 1960 that the hotel was hoping to grow its convention business from $3 million to $5 million each year. Alas, the center of gravity for Chicago's convention business had shifted downtown with the opening of the McCormick Place Convention Center, observed industry veteran John Monahan.

While the years after World War II were America's most prosperous, they also spelled the beginning of the end for the old-world elegance epitomized by the Edgewater Beach Hotel. Perhaps the most striking example of this shift was the construction south of the hotel of a new lodging complex, the Sands Motel. Despite leveraging its proximity to the hotel, the Sands was a decidedly more downscale lodging experience. Contrasted with the hotel's Olympic-sized pool surrounded by a landscaped cabana complex, the Sands offered a small swimming pool amidst a sea of parking, a common feature of motels from the 1950s and 1960s.

Eight

THE END AND THE LEGACY

By the mid-1960s, especially observant visitors might have detected signs of neglect cropping up around the Edgewater Beach Hotel. Peeling paint in rooms and common areas was just one manifestation. Entire floors of the hotel were also closed due to a lack of business and maintenance. This decline seemed to have accelerated after the hotel was sold again in 1962.

Still, Chicago citizens and hotel residents were caught by surprise when management announced the abrupt closure of the hotel two days before Christmas 1967—and that the hotel would close the next day. The following year, the hotel took on a brief second life when it was used as a temporary dormitory by nearby Loyola University. The pool and cabana complex also enjoyed a brief afterlife following the hotel's closure in response to community demands, and special memberships were sold to the pool complex.

Still, when plans for a series of new high-rise apartment towers on the site emerged from developer Marshall Holleb, there was no turning back the bulldozers. Buildings that were meant for the ages were now targeted for demolition a mere 40 to 50 years after being constructed. Following the closure, the grand dame was left to an ignoble end. An auction was held to sell off anything in the hotel—from linens to doorknobs—that could bring in extra cash. These items still have a vigorous afterlife for collectors around the world. After the auction, the hotel property was left unsecured, and many urban adventurers were able to access it to have a last look at the grand old place before the wreckers arrived.

Chicago's nascent historic preservation movement had yet to get on its feet before the Edgewater Beach Hotel was consigned to the ash heap of history. Had the move to demolish come just a few years later, perhaps there would have been more of a fight to save it. Coincidentally, 1967 was the year that another beloved Chicago institution—the Riverview amusement park—also abruptly closed, another victim of the changing times.

However, the solidity of the Edgewater Beach Hotel's construction would have the last laugh at the developers who wanted to be rid of it. A job slated to take six months wound up taking thirteen, and the last pile of rubble was not carted away until April 1971.

Perhaps nothing signaled the hotel's change of direction in the 1960s more than when Teamsters Union president Jimmy Hoffa took up semiregular residence in a suite that reportedly cost $1,000 per day. The Edgewater Beach became a principal spot for national meetings of the teamsters at a time when they were enmeshed in some of their toughest negotiations and also when the federal government was preparing to indict Hoffa. Regulars of the hotel report that Hoffa's security detail and other hangers-on were often seen roughhousing in the hotel's lobbies, which definitely did not help the hotel's fraying sense of elegance.

We've been in the hotel business for over 40 years. Never yet have we called the police to eject a disorderly dog during the small hours of the night. Never yet has a dog set the bedclothes afire from smoking a cigarette. We've never found a hotel towel or blanket in a dog's suitcase, no whiskey rings on the bureau top from a dog's bottle. Sure the dog's welcome!

EDGEWATER BEACH HOTEL

p.s.   If he'll vouch for you, you
        can come, too.

Perhaps it was extremely progressive management that prompted this change, or perhaps it was a sign that business was lagging at the hotel, and it was willing to adopt policies that might bring in new business. Whatever the reason, the hotel was definitely decades ahead of its time with its dog-friendly stance shown in this promotional card. The implication that dogs might be less trouble than some human guests may have hinted at the decline in the class of some clientele.

Minsky's Follies was an updated American take on the old Folies Bergere formula of burlesque featuring dancing girls baring ample amounts of skin. It was a mainstay for years in Las Vegas and had an extended run at the Edgewater Beach Hotel's reconstituted Marine Dining Room in what proved to be the hotel's final summer in 1967.

Though the Minsky's Follies shows tended to attract mainstream audiences, it was nevertheless a slightly tawdry departure for the elegant old hotel to be presenting such programming. For decades, William Dewey ran the hotel with a strict moral code that did not tolerate unmarried couples sharing rooms or unaccompanied women entering the hotel's bars. Dewey undoubtedly would not have been happy that the hotel was now featuring "nudie" shows.

While the hotel labored on, its finances apparently continued to deteriorate, and maintenance at the hotel was increasingly being deferred. Entire floors were closed, though employees reported that business was still quite brisk until the end. For owner H.P. Weissberg, who acquired the hotel in 1962, bankruptcy court was looming along with $6 million in outstanding debt. Chicago attorney and developer Marshall Holleb was waiting in the wings to grab the prized real estate in the proceedings. Holleb is shown here with legendary Chicago planning commissioner Ira Bach (left) discussing plans for the redevelopment of the property.

This image shows the Edgewater Beach Hotel campus and surrounding community in early 1968. On the north end (at left), the first tower of the Edgewater Plaza complex is visible. It was built on the land where the tennis courts had been and was sold off separately prior to the bankruptcy. At the time, the neighborhood west of Sheridan Road was in steep urban decline, adding to the woes of the hotel.

Perhaps fittingly, Chicago-born comic and storyteller George Gobel was the last performer to appear on stage at the Edgewater Beach Hotel. Gobel's hangdog "perpetual loser" routine seems to have subtly reflected the mood that hung over the hotel in its final months. This playbill also shows that bittersweet chanteuse Peggy Lee was scheduled to appear weeks after the hotel's abrupt closing, depriving the grand old hotel of a swan song of Lee's "Is That All There Is?"

On the afternoon of December 22, 1967, the hotel's 65 permanent residents were informed that the hotel was closing immediately and they would have to move within 24 hours, just days before Christmas. Transient guests of the hotel were told to leave by the end of the day. Here, Cora Brown—who had lived in the hotel for more than 40 years, since it first welcomed permanent residents—processes the news with the hotel's staff.

The hotel got one last turn at hosting in 1968, when Loyola University leased it as a residence for 500 students while the school awaited the completion of a new dormitory. In a development that also might have raised one of William Dewey's eyebrows, it was Loyola's first coed student housing. Many students were charmed by the old-world elegance their temporary living arrangements afforded. One of the perks the arrangement offered to the residents was that the hotel's Presidential Suite was used as a student lounge. Note this corporate-style entrance canopy that replaced the hotel's picturesque portico.

A year after the pool opened in 1953, a series of double-decked cabanas were built around three sides of the pool. The cabanas provided guests with a place to change into their beachwear without going into the hotel. Curiously, the pool actually outlasted the hotel by a year. For the 1968 summer season, the hotel's owners continued to generate cash flow for the bankrupt hotel by selling private pool memberships that included a dedicated cabana.

Adding pressure on the hotel was the sharp decline of the surrounding community, with many of the once-elegant homes chopped up for rooming houses and altered for commercial uses, as shown here. This area was significantly revitalized after hitting its bottom in the 1980s.

This image shows the early stages of the demolition of the original tower, which commenced in January 1970. Incredulous and sometimes teary-eyed spectators came from across the metro area to get final glimpses at and photographs of the ruins of the once-elegant oasis. The first of the two Edgewater Plaza buildings is visible at right. The new high-rise buildings that replaced the hotel were able to offer lakefront living for thousands of additional residents but at the expense of the unique and graceful experience once offered by the Edgewater Beach Hotel.

Demolition of the hotel was expected to take six months. Cleveland-based Boyas Excavating Company got the wrecking contract. "It looks like a more complicated wrecking job than it is," said owner Pete Boyas. He learned the hard way that it would take 13 months. George Stanton observed, "I remember when they were building it and I remember the sad days when they had to tear it down floor by floor. . . . An atom bomb wouldn't have brought it down—they criss-crossed the steel beams so well. An earthquake might have cracked the walls . . . but it would never fall down." Demolition was not completed until 1971. Designed to last centuries, the complex—once a bragging point for Chicago—succumbed to the wrecking ball after barely more than 50 years. Chicago's historic preservation movement was just getting started at the time. "Buildings like the Edgewater Beach were much loved . . . but were almost secondary to what was being lost at the time," observed Ward Miller, president of Preservation Chicago. Many of Chicago's great train stations and Louis Sullivan designs were also being wrecked.

The year 1971 saw not only the completion of the demolition of the Edgewater Beach Hotel but also the destruction of Benjamin Marshall's Edgewater Gulf in Mississippi. Perhaps aware of how arduous the demolition of the Edgewater Beach was, the owners of the Edgewater Gulf elected to implode that structure. Even that did not go as planned; two additional blasts were needed to complete the job.

Initial plans for the former Edgewater Beach Hotel property called for a complex of three triangular steel and black glass apartment towers, each reaching more than 50 stories. Reminiscent of Benjamin Marshall's failure to fully execute on his original grandiose plans for the site, Marshall Holleb succeeded in building only one of the three towers, the 54-story Park Tower (left). Much of the land sat empty until the Breakers retirement community (right) and a series of townhomes were constructed in the 1980s by different developers.

A huge auction of items from the Edgewater Beach Hotel was held shortly before demolition work began on the hotel. A crowd of more than 2,000 interested buyers showed up. Everything from furniture to matchbooks was sold off to a mournful public who wanted a lasting piece of the hotel that had meant so much to them. The legacy of the hotel still lives on in countless collections of memorabilia held around the world. This is a random assortment of hotel china, programs, menus, and other ephemera from the collection of the Edgewater Historical Society.

EDGEWATER BEACH HOTEL · CHICAGO ·

While the world of the Edgewater Beach Hotel is now just a memory, it continues to be an inspiration for those who contemplate its glories. This impressionistic image was from a series of paintings showing the hotel at its grandest. The Edgewater Beach Hotel might also have been the only hotel to have inspired a poem. Below is an excerpt from "To the Edgewater Beach Hotel" by Fannie B. Linderman:

A Queen you stand majestic,
The waters bathe your feet;
Your towers stretch far towards Heaven,
Your beauty never wavers
To hearts attuned to thee,
O! Edgewater, proud and beauteous,
Bride of an inland sea. . . .
In all your changing seasons,
Your anchor holds me fast;
QUEEN of our own great city,
Long may thy kingdom last

DISCOVER THOUSANDS OF LOCAL HISTORY BOOKS
FEATURING MILLIONS OF VINTAGE IMAGES

Arcadia Publishing, the leading local history publisher in the United States, is committed to making history accessible and meaningful through publishing books that celebrate and preserve the heritage of America's people and places.

Find more books like this at
www.arcadiapublishing.com

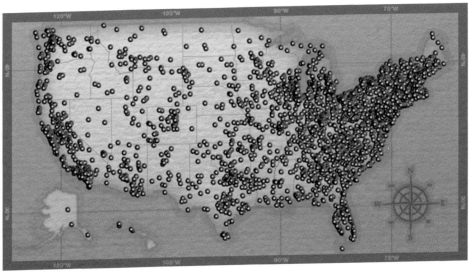

Search for your hometown history, your old stomping grounds, and even your favorite sports team.

Consistent with our mission to preserve history on a local level, this book was printed in South Carolina on American-made paper and manufactured entirely in the United States. Products carrying the accredited Forest Stewardship Council (FSC) label are printed on 100 percent FSC-certified paper.

MADE IN THE USA